GOD, FAMILY, THE FUTURE, THE PRESENT,
SILENCE, ADVENTURE, THE WORLD,
TIME, UNKNOWN, MY HEART, MY SOUL, MY
MIND, COLLEGE, JOB, MY PAIN, MY JOY,
MY STRENGTH, THOUGHTS, THE DEVIL,
REST, CHURCH, THE BEACH, DEATH,
ADDICTION, PRIDE, MEMORIES, TITI,
HARD-WORK, LOVE, JOY, BETRAYAL, SEEDS,
ABANDONMENT, LIES, TRUTH, BEAUTY,
THE POWER OF A VOICE, PEACE, THE
CITY, OVERFLOWING, FIGHTING, FREEDOM,
WEALTH, WISHING, PRESUMPTIONS,
DEPRESSION, OPPRESSION, ATTENDANCE,
RUNNING, SETTLING, HUSTLE, LAVENDER,
TRAVELING, THE SEA, LETTING GO,
FORGIVENESS, MIRACLES, PRAYER,
DOUBT, PITTY, AIRPLANES, PRESSING,
SELF-HEALING, THE SIGNS, WAITING,
REVELATION, HATTIE, REALIZATIONS,
EDUCATION, TIME, CROWNS, HEAVEN,
TREES, JUSTICE, THE PERFECTION
GLASS, INSECURITIES, RIDICULE

THE

PAPER AIRPLANE

EFFECT

Volume 1:

The Good, Bad, & Ugly of Transparency

By: Alexander Berry

AKA: Old Soul

<u>Change Me</u>

I'm tired of the same old me, the broken
me. I am ready and willing to accept the new
me. So go ahead God, I'll tear down my barriers
and allow you to move how you please. I accept
the "me" you want me to be. I desperately need
and want you to change me. I understand change
is hard, uncomfortable, and sometimes awkward.
Regardless, I'll continue to push on in allowing
you to change me. I keep in mind the end goal,
the happy ending. Most importantly I remember
the good you were, are, and continue to work out
for me.

Sincerely,

The Old Me

A Simple Command

God doesn't make us do anything. He loves us regardless of our flaws and mistakes, but He doesn't want us to wallow in them. He sets standards. He has things He wants and requires us to do:

1. Love the Lord God with all your heart, soul, mind and strength. (Mark 12:30, Matthew 22:37, Deuteronomy 6:5, and Luke 10:27)

2. Love your neighbor as yourself. (Mark 12:34)

Later on in the Bible, God tells us to love one another as God loves us, therefore love one another. He said that probably because He knew some people do not love themselves, but in putting that in the Bible we have no excuse to not love, because He loves without boarders or limitations. There is no excuse to not love it's just that simple.

Sincerely,

Lover

God Provides

Though sometimes it looks like God isn't doing something, those moments were created to test your faith. Our faith can't survive on just things we see, it requires us to believe in what we can't see. Sometimes we need to stop fighting and just sit down and watch God provide. God will provide above and beyond what we want, need, or ask for IF we allow Him. It may not always appear on our time schedule but it will appear at the right time. When you have no food, you can't pay the bills, you're struggling physically and emotionally, watch God provide and then praise Him for bringing you through the storm.

Sincerely,

Someone provided for

Waiting at Locked Doors

Sometimes God puts us in a waiting period. Imagine you're sitting in a chair and you're surrounded by doors. Each door is different; different colors, styles, some old, some new, some elaborate and ornate, some simple, but they're all locked. When sitting earnestly awaiting for the unknown I call that, "The Waiting Period" and the doors are the doors that God opens and shuts. When God is ready for you to walk through a door He'll unlock and open it but until then we are to wait. God said, "He works all things for good to those who love the Lord" (Romans 8:28). If one loves God they obey God when He tells them to wait (John 14:15). God is constantly working the good out for us. Have you ever thought about what's on the other side of those doors? Here in the natural when a house or building is under construction or renovation the door is locked for your protection. There may be a hole in the ground, nails on the floor, a loose board, or worse. It's the same in the spiritual. When a door is closed think, "Wow, thank you God for going ahead," because maybe He's fixing the floor, cleaning up the nails, and other stuff so you're not always walking into a mess but a blessing

instead. We sometimes like to force our way into
a situation. We get tired of waiting on God and
let our natural situation control us rather than
waiting on God. So we decide to kick in the door
and tell God "NOT LATER, NOW." We make our own
way while we wave our little finger around in the
air telling God how to do things, but then when
you fall through the hole in the floor and get a
nail in your foot, after tripping over that loose
board don't blame God for not warning you or not
doing "His Job" blame yourself. God doesn't
bless disobedience, He blesses humility and
obedience.

Don't let outward situations and
circumstances determine inward decisions. You
may be wondering what are the loose boards, hole
in the floor and nails on the ground behind the
door in the spiritual and how they correlate to
the physical natural world. That's your terrible
job where all the drama is, the situations you
put yourself in that are a complete disaster,
it's everything that you forced out of God's will
and out of God's time. It's okay to wait, it may
be scary, seem crazy, look stupid, but it leads
to something much better.

Sincerely,

A Person in Waiting

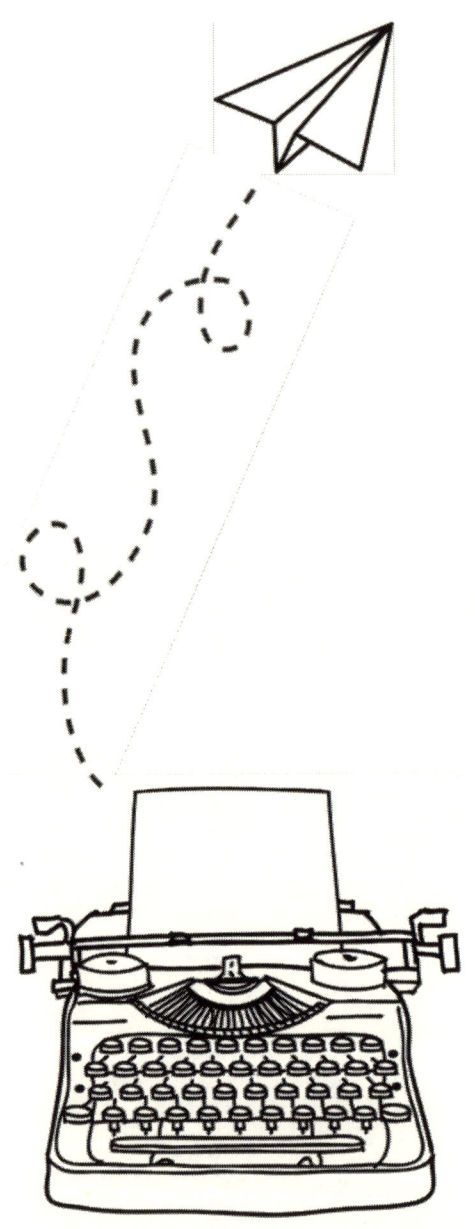

"Hurt people hurt people,

Broken people break people,

But the bigger person forgives,

Moves on and loves anyways"

- Old Soul

Fix Me

Please, I'm desperately seeking
and yearning for you to fix me
so the future won't have to know the broken me.
Oh, fix me.

Fix my crooked thinking,
my twisted thoughts,
my wicked wonders.
Oh, fix me.

Fix my broken heart,
that is bruised and crying
so that I may love easier.
Fix Me.

I set my guard down,
my walls I break down,
and my arms I outreach.
Fix Me.

Forgive the actions of the broken me.
I surrender myself entirely
to your miracle working hands.
I come to the end of myself
So I can come to the beginning of you.
Fix Me.

Fix me from the top to the bottom.
I won't stop you this time.
Please fix me.

Find the Positive Change

What's your outlook like? We can choose
to look at the negative or the positive. This
is especially important to look at and check
when walking into a new season of life. Change
is uncomfortable and scary, but it's all a part
of it. You can look at the negative of change
or try to find the good. Negative things like
to stick out so they can make us sad, mad,
angry, bitter, and break down our faith. You
have to put forth the effort to find the positive
sometimes. It's hard but there's always a
positive, ALWAYS. So, today and every day from
now on embrace change with a positive outlook and
act in the positive.

Sincerely,

Someone Changing

<u>Live Again</u>

      Sometimes God has to send fire to burn away things so new life can grow. Sometimes God sends a bomb from heaven to blow away things and obstructions in the way so new life can grow. We all have a river of life within us that He wants uncovered and to flow freely. God is willing to get everything out of the way however only He can, but only if we want Him to. God sends bombs to blow away the materials in the way so our geysers of life can burst forth without limitations. God wants our rivers to flow without limitations or borders so it can flow into every area of our life, our neighbors, our community, our family, our friends. He wants to give our land life again. He wants to take the dry land of our hearts and fill it with life once again. He wants us to grow and to flourish, that's why He puts a river on the inside of us, but it does us no good if we clog it up with our own ways. Let the river flow, burst out of its borders and expand into every area of our life.

Sincerely,

Land

Find the Positive

Instead of always finding the negative in someone how about we search for the positive. Everyday find and point out the positive in everything. Though sometimes someone may look absolutely terrible, still find one good thing. That positive thing that you pointed out may make that person's day or may even save their life. A positive word can make just as much impact as a negative one if taken to heart the same way. Sometimes when someone compliments us we reason the kindness out of it. We think they're out to get us, they're forced to say that because they're related to me, or they're being sarcastic. WHO CARES? The best way to defeat any of those things is to just take the compliment and act as if it was the most genuine thing in the world. There is always a reason to be positive whether you feel like it or not. Fake it 'til you make it.

Sincerely,

Someone trying to be Optimistic

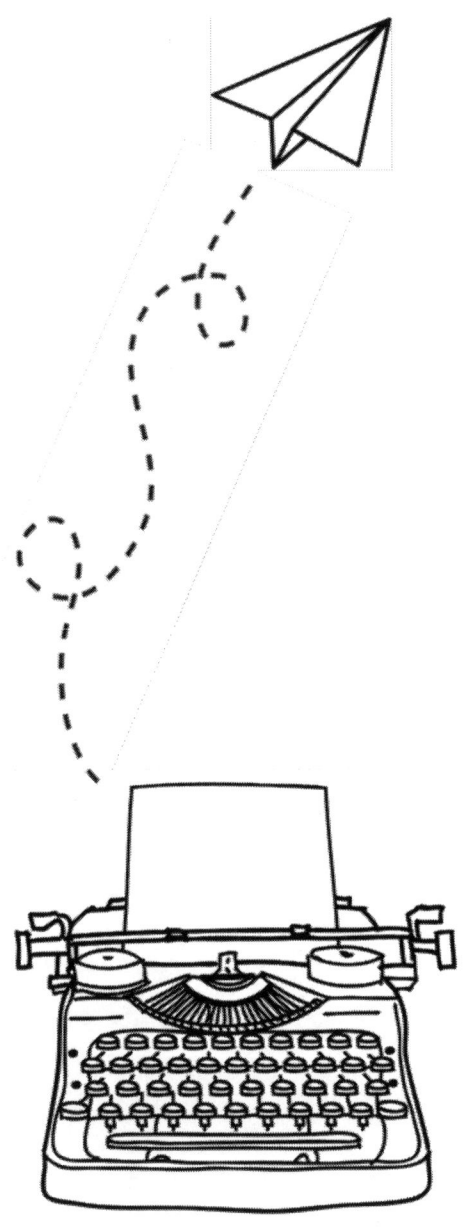

"I'm starting with the man in the mirror"

~ Michael Jackson

Hold Your Tongue

In our very tongue we hold the power to kill, destroy, distance and erode away the very existence of a person. Our words describe our understanding of something whether it is a person, place or thing and or our connotation towards it. The power of our words is stronger than any force on earth. We were given this power for good but some use it to destroy. It's crazy and hard to believe we could erase the very existence and remembrance of any person. Let me explain...

Imagine someone makes you extremely mad so you decide to tell everyone the negative about that person and shine a negative light towards that person with everyone you come in contact with. So now, not only do you not like this person but everyone you've talked to about that person now either doesn't like them or is leery of them. That person now has an entire army of people against them and may now have no one supporting them. So lost and trapped in these thoughts of malice this person decides they don't deserve to live and kills themselves. Now you can be considered as a murderer, and because that one thing they said still bothers you, you continue to talk bad about that person and make everyone who feels bad for that person feel bad themselves. Over time the thoughts and memories of that person fade, generations go by and their name and life is forgotten. Suddenly, everyone's memory of that person, even if they did everything right, saved lives, and did as much good as possible, is all erased. It's all erased because they provoked your ego and you couldn't take it. You couldn't brush it off; you just had to get the upper hand.

On the other hand, your mouth could be the babbling brook of which words of life spring forth. People come to you to draw from your wells the words of wisdom and inspiration of which you freely offer. Your words could be the words that bring life to another's dried up, dead, and God forsaken land. Your prayers shoot forth ministering angels that go forth and bring healing, deliverance, life, prosperity, salvation, and freedom. Your words could spread life and joy, peace and love, justice and safety. Your words can only do so if you let them. It's a conscience decision you have to make. How will you use your words today, tomorrow, or next week? Will you let other people determine what kind of water flows from your well?

Sincerely,

A Word Guardian

Possible Dreams

From Impossible Thoughts

There's a certain happiness that you receive when you see your dreams and aspirations come true in ways you didn't think possible. God has this certain way of doing the otherwise impossible and in turn He shows Himself great. Just when you think you have Him all figured out you find another layer. Things you said could never happen, all of a sudden start happening. If we trust God, He will do the unimaginable. I thought I couldn't be a teacher until after I earned a degree in 5 years, but I graduated high school and at the startup of the next school year I was a teacher's aide for K-4. That is God proving the possible in the impossible.

Sincerely,

Victim of the impossible turned possible

<u>Proven Wrong</u>

God has this funny way of proving some people wrong. It manifests in different ways than would be expected. He says in Matthew 20:16, "so the last shall be first and the first shall be last." When the world throws you to the back, signs you up for failure, writes you off, and doubts you, God is doing the opposite. God will pull you to the front, give you victory, bless you, and is constantly excited to see you succeed. Even when you give up on yourself, God is busy loving you and cheering you on. God declares that you are the head and not the tail, above only and not beneath regardless of what the world says.

Sincerely,

A Victory Possessor

End of the Road

It's true what they say, "When you come to the end of the road God can begin." We need to come to the end of ourselves so we can allow God to take complete control. You get to the point eventually where you can't handle it anymore and you have to give it to God, which is what He has wanted all along. We were never meant to walk the road alone or carry everything. God wants us to give it to Him and walk in unity with Him. His burden is easy and His yoke is light. Meaning what He wants us to carry is easy and manageable, and the work we do, when done with Him is easy to accomplish.

Sincerely,

Someone at the End

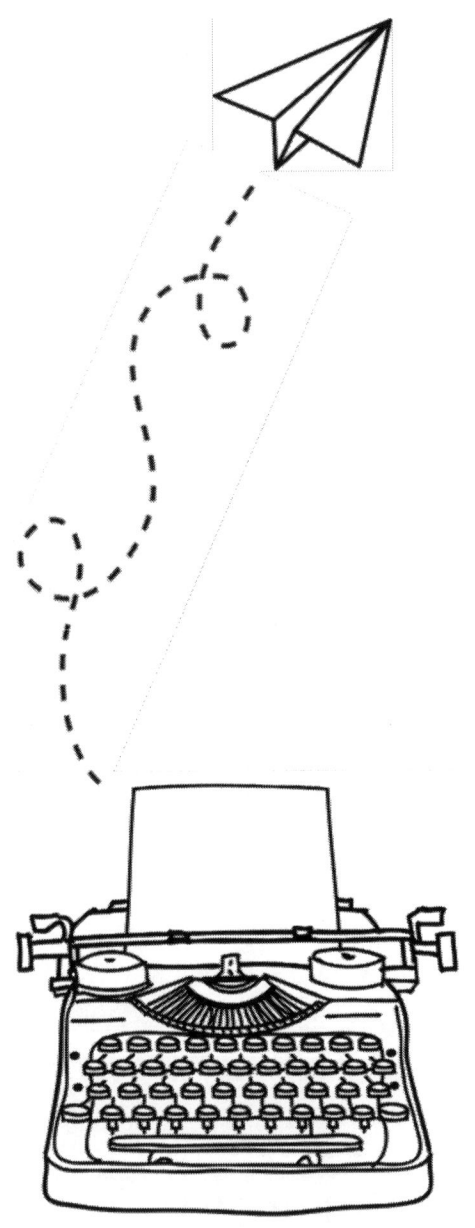

"It's better to travel and get lost...

than never to travel at all."

~ Anonymous

Relax and Trust

I got your back. I'll handle your
problems, your situations, and your enemies.
Just Relax. Trust that I got you. Lay here in
my arms, hear My heartbeat, feel My love. If
you stay here with Me I'll take care of it all.
Become one with Me, let our hearts sync up; let
our emotions, aspirations, and motives be the
same. Let us move as one. Find peace in Me and
trust that I do what is best for you. I always
have the best in mind for you, regardless of what
it may look like, feel like, or even seem like.
Forget it all and focus on Me. Let Me take you
to the "Beyond". Let Me transcend you beyond
your problems, come with Me in perfect peace.
Trust that I'll open the right door. Just walk
in with great hope. Don't let others determine
what I am. Lay here in My arms. Let Me draw you
closer. Hold onto this: I know what's to come.
I love you. Trust Me regardless of what people
say.

I love you,

Papa

<u>Running to you</u>

It's time. Time to run in the right
direction. I'm running straight to you. I
finally realize that it's you I've been looking
for. I'm not holding back this time. Your arms
are outreached and I'm leaping into them. The
years of running against Your current are over
and the years of flowing with them begin. I'll
let you sweep me off my feet and sail me to new
pastures and levels. Accelerate me to new
wisdom. I'm realizing that to run with you is
much easier than running against you.

Sincerely,

The Runner

Surrounded, Please

When it looks like the walls are high and they're all against me I realize I'm surrounded by You. Angels are encamped all around me. No weapon formed against me shall prosper. I am surrounded by You. You set me in a large place then surrounded me, not to lock me in but to keep my enemies out. This is how I fight my battles, with arms outstretched and with your direction. The enemy thinks he has me surrounded but the Lord is surrounding me and he will have to get through God first. Yeah I'm surrounded, but not by you devil but by God.

We as Christians see the small surrounding the devil has around us, yet fail to see the HUGE barricade that is unbreakable that the Lord put around us.

Sincerely,

Someone with Heavenly Surroundings

It Planted a Seed

Everything you say to yourself or to someone else plants a seed of good or bad. When you talk about someone negatively to another person you've then planted a seed of negative connotation towards that person you're talking about. How you talk to your child for instance is the type of fruit you will see grow as they get older. This is why you have to be careful of who you surround yourself with on a daily basis. Imagine we are all gardeners preparing gardens. In one hand you have seeds of beautiful fruit and flowers and in the other hand you have seeds of thorns and weeds, it's your choice which seeds you'll spread. No one can make you do anything. If you want to see the good grow in your life you must first plant it, water it, and tend to it. You also have to make sure that you are constantly tending to your garden, killing and uprooting weeds, pulling out dead or diseased plants in order to maintain the overall survival of the entire garden. No one can ever just plant something in your garden unless you allow it.

Sincerely,

A Garden Himself

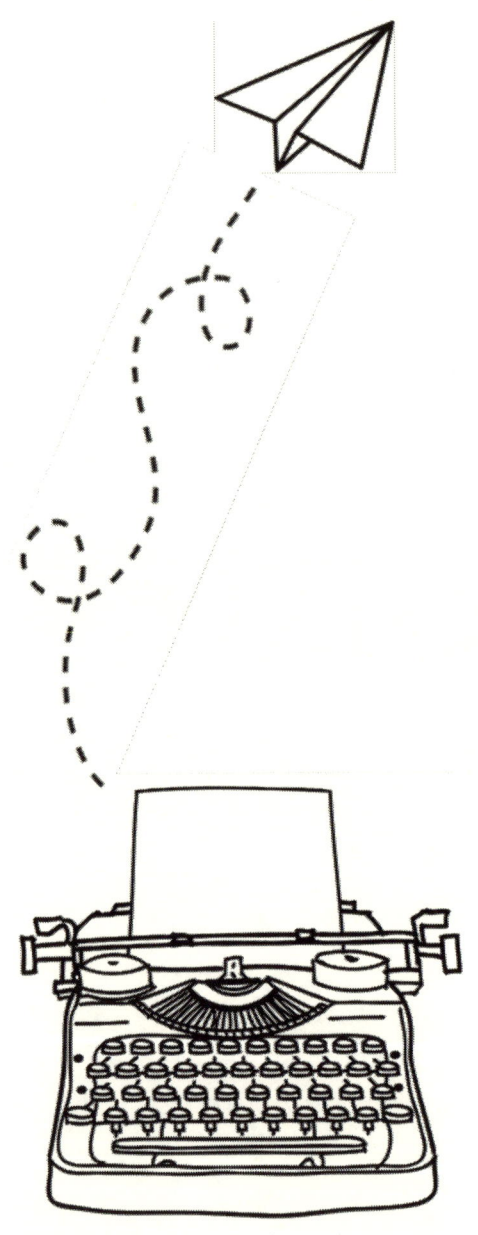

"Enjoy the little things in life,
for someday you will realize
they were the BIG THINGS"

- Kurt Vonnegut

Having it All

Just because you have it all doesn't mean that you have it all. Just because you have all the material things and it looks like your life is together doesn't mean it is. Just because people see that you have a cookie-cutter life and think that your life is perfect that doesn't mean it's true. You can have it all but still be emotionally empty with no morals, no standards, nothing to grow from and nothing to stand firm on. You can be someone that is broken, hurting, and struggling on the inside. People can tell you that you're spoiled and that everything is handed to you on a "Silver Platter" without ever knowing what has been going on behind the scenes.

Have you ever thought that maybe God gave that person those things, a good life, material objects, all just to prove to that person how good He really is. Maybe that person is still broken and has been mistreated and hurt throughout the years and God needed some way to physically show that person that He does care, He does see them, that He notices their pain and hurt, and that He does truly love them. He has counted their tears and felt their pain. He would give the world for that person just to let them know they are loved. He would spoil them with the riches of the world to show them that He will spoil them with the riches of Heaven. There are no limitations to His powers, there's no understanding His knowledge. That is why it's said that He will make a way out of no way. People may not understand how that person received those things but the very people who hurt them gave it to them. Those that hurt you and mistreat you may one day be the same people that are serving you in the end. A perfect example of this is Joseph with his brothers. Read Genesis 37 in the bible and you will see that they made his life terrible then later in life returned begging for his help. In that moment Joseph had to decide what example he would be. It is up to us to decide the course of our lives whether we will choose to love or to hate, the power is in us. It's never them who decides, it is always us.

Also, just because it looks like someone is getting away with something does not mean that they are. God has our back. He is our Father. He won't let them get away with anything. He has a purpose for you and a purpose for them. He is demonstrating His working power through people in ways that we do not always see or understand.

Sincerely,

Someone who has had it all

The Paper Airplane

   Sometimes we don't want to admit it but it
may be time to move on. We need to embrace the
time to change. It's a time to let the wind set
our planes into flight. We may not know where
we're going but that's the best part. Take the
time to float in the wind and let it take you to
the next landing spot. When we land we should
evaluate our surroundings with a willingness
to learn. It may not seem like a place where
we would want to be but we're there to learn
something. We should embrace the lessons no
matter how big or small. You'll know within when
it's time to take flight. Everything will start
to line up, you'll feel the release, and before
you know it... whoosh. You've taken flight.
You'll land once again in areas in which lessons
are to be learned and memories made. People will
think you're crazy, but all the best people are.

   Now, don't get me wrong. We do sometimes
get the false feeling of takeoff. We want out
of something because it no longer tickles our
fancy or we get bored. So we start trying to
make things line up ourselves. We try to set
ourselves into flight mode and push ourselves off
the ground, but just when you feel like you're

flying... BANG! You hit the ground. WHY? Because you cannot force the wind to blow in a direction when it's not time. We are forced back into learning the same lesson all over again because we either didn't get it the first time or we disregard and disvalue its importance and we need that lesson under our belt in order to take flight again. Sometimes we continuously ignore the lesson and we still wonder why we can't take flight to new places. You may not be in the same physical place, but recognize that wherever you go you still have to learn that lesson. While in a place as a paper airplane we should share our stories. It may help someone with the lesson that they are learning, motivate someone to keep flying, or even inspire them. Our planes are our lives, our stories, and our lessons learned. They are what make us unique, and give us character. They should be available to be read and to learn from. I'm proud of my paper plane. Are you?

Sincerely,

A Paper Airplane

Boundaries

When people hear the word broken they automatically have a negative connotation. But what about the things that are supposed to be broken like cookies so they can fit into milk. No, seriously think about it. Limits and boundaries are meant to be broken. We should search for the next great thing. Where to next? We should never get to a point in our my lives where we're just complacent. Satisfied with a mediocre day-to-day, unexciting, uneventful job should never be the goal.

Every now and then we need to take some time to ourselves, and evaluate where we are in life. While doing so we should answer these 3 simple questions:

1) What are my limitations?

2) What are my dreams?

3) What is stopping me from achieving?

Surpass your limitations leaving all doubt behind you. Strive to achieve more than anyone thinks of you or you think of yourself. If you have met all your goals in life then set new ones and keep a visible log of them that way you can't forget them. So what's the next boundary that needs to broken?

Sincerely,
A Boundary Breaker

At the Bottom

It was there,

the bottom where we met,

the bottom where are hearts connect.

I hit rock bottom and like the strike of two rocks

A spark...

Boom...

it lit a candle that reflected light,

it illuminated and gave sight.

If only the devil knew what was to come, my insight

He just brought to light.

The space around me still,

and at the bottom I found me

As horrible as I was to me,

He was the one who saved me.

Pushed me towards my destiny,

pulled me from the animosity,

and showed me who I could be.

Who I could've been,

Who I was set up to be,

Who I should've been.

But in the reflection of me I saw...
it wouldn't be me,
I would be free.
I was set apart to see
deliberately.

In the mirror I saw myself
back to back with Serenity.
The One who created me,
The One who formed me,
The One who breathed life into me
and said this one will change the course of
history.

The One who saw me,
acknowledged me,
prospered me.
The One who said in the end it's just you and me
because at the bottom the Foundation was truly
Me.

Dealing with the root it's between you and Me.

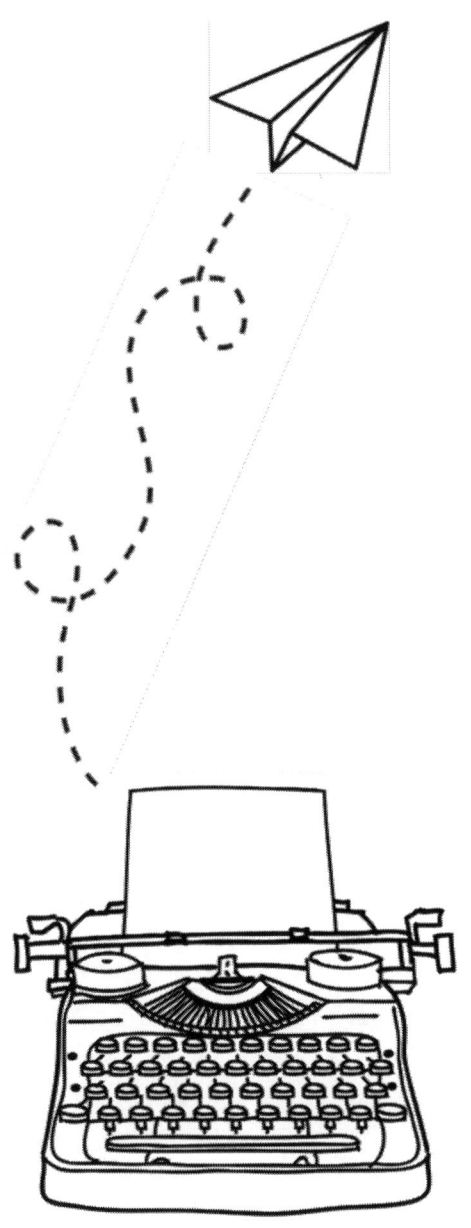

"You never fail until

you stop trying"

~ Albert Einstein

PERFECTION GLASS

I feel like I went from being a little kid to being thrown and forced into adulthood. For years I felt like I had to be perfect. Don't mess up. Don't trip up. Be perfect. Constantly, I felt the need to bury any imperfection or emotions I had. My voice was nothing but a mere interruption in others' plans and vision for my life. Any time I didn't perform exactly to the "T" of their plan, I let them down, they were disappointed or ashamed of me and I was a disappointment.

My mind never let a day go by where it didn't speak the following to me:

"No one loves an imperfect person. People don't love brokenness, they love perfection and you are broken. You will never be able to love someone and they will never be able to love you until you first fix yourself and your imperfections. Boy, do you have a lot to fix inside and out! Look at you. Now think about yourself internally. You are so broken and damaged, it's impossible to fix you. BURY IT ALL. You have a reputation to uphold and your brokenness is unacceptable. You will be rejected and an outcast if you break the PERFECTION GLASS

in which people see you through. Oops too late.
Your perfection glass has cracks. Hurry fix it!
Make sure people don't see your flaws. Remember,
people loving you, liking you, approving of
you it's all on the line. Don't Mess Up. You
are expected to do everything right and if you
don't YOU ARE A FAILURE. Keep in mind others'
expectations, they are what matter. To mess
up is to be rejected. To shatter the GLASS is
to be rejected. Conceal your heart into the
deepest corner because it's so broken. Nobody
wants to see that, hear that, love that. People
don't want to love you; they want to love your
PERFECTION GLASS. You are a young immature child
and nobody wants to hear you, your opinion, or
anything you have to say. So shut up. Perform
inside the realm of the PERFECTION GLASS, shut
up and don't mess up. What don't you understand
about that? Gosh you really are stupid!"

My heart longed to just be a teenager. Do
dumb teenager things. Live like all the other
teenagers. But that didn't fit within others'
expectations and standards for me. My whole life
I've strived to please everyone, but when will I
be good enough? Others say, "Oh please, you've
lived a very full life as a teenager." To them I
have because I've done it all within their cookie
cutter mold for me, my life, and my dreams. I've
done it all inside the walls of the PERFECTION
GLASS. I slipped a little outside the mold once
and my heart had to suffer. People made it very

clear that I cracked the PERFECTION GLASS and
turned on me. Some say I'm presumptuous, but
after seeking people's approval all my life, I
know the look and tone of disapproval. The sad
part is I know it all too well. So here I am
still hearing my mind's story while striving
to keep the PERFECTION GLASS looking spotless.
Congratulations everyone, the forever damage
is done although you'll never see it. I will
never get to be a normal teenager. Never live
some childhood dreams of what it's like to be a
teenager. Never experience what's supposed to be
the greatest time of my life because I spent it
all being squeezed inside the PERFECTION GLASS.
The saddest part is I never even got the chance.
I officially went from little child to adult. Who
cares, but yet why would anyone care?

But hey, at least you have your PERFECTION
GLASS.

Sincerely,

PERFECTION GLASS
(a prisoner)

Relentless

God's love is relentless and I saw in my mind's eye God sending out His Son. He's running relentlessly to find us pushing over anything and everything in the way to get to us. There wasn't a limit He wouldn't break just to get to us. HE WOULD NOT STOP. Nothing we could do or say would stop Him. He saw us crying in the corner feeling so lonely and that only motivated Him so much more. He knew what we had been through, are going through and will go through and it never stopped Him. He just ran faster and faster and faster. RELENTLESSLY. TIRELESSLY. EARNESTLY. RECKLESSLY. There's a song that talks about this and it goes as such:

There's no shadow You won't light up

Mountain You won't climb up

Coming after me

There's no wall you won't kick down

No lie you won't tear down

Coming after me

He desires to just wrap us in His arms but some hold Him at arms distance refusing the tight embrace of Love Himself that we so longingly desire. We prevent ourselves from obtaining

love, and going to greater levels in Him. On
the other hand some embrace the hug of love and
transcend with Him to achieve the unbelievable.
He knows our limits and our strengths. He knew
when to push us to strive for more (because we
weren't giving it our all) and when to just
simply embrace us. He knew when to make us fight
and when to put us into perfect peace and fight
the battle for us. He loves us so recklessly
that He doesn't care what other people think of
Him or His love. He cares about our connection
to Him because His goal, His one goal is simply
love (and maybe crush the devil in the process).
Love us, love all, simply love and there is
nothing He would not do to love us all.

Sincerely,

A Victim of Reckless Love

I'm Not Staying

Every day I walked in my self-worth
diminished all by the words of one. I dreaded
the days I would have to see their face. Fear,
sadness, rage, drained, and stupid are just some
words that being around them made you feel. How
can one feel any different when that's all they
hear all day by you? Your words were sharper
than knives and heavier than the biggest boulder.
They dug deep tearing down every last drop of
one's confidence. For what? To make you feel
better about yourself. You would rather make
someone feel completely worthless and still beat
them down to prove an invalid point. You made
me cry by your words, and leave by your actions.
Push, push, pushed too far. You broke us all.
Outside we didn't show it. We wouldn't show
it. We wouldn't let you win. But inside bits
and pieces of our hearts had been shattered. We
banded together because we realized it's the only
way we would survive. Our time lost on empty
promises and crushed hope. You made me question
my existence by convincing me I was stupid. No
smarter than a five year old, a baby even. You
thought that saying I was "to skinny" didn't hurt
me, but over time it hit deeper and deeper and
deeper until finally my very core started to cry.
You drove my mind to the knife and my heart to

62

the cliff, but I'm stronger now. And you? You're broken and we all see it. We all see you for who you really are. Broken with very little self-worth, striving to overcompensate for the lack there of by tearing down everyone else. Maybe it wasn't us that were always wrong and too

stupid to realize the obvious. Maybe had you listened to us, talked to us, and thought before you spoke to us we would all still be here. But yet, your ego got in the way and took precedence over anything else. You put yourself over others leading to your own demise. Like they say, "You can't treat people like dogs and expect them to stay around and love you." That's not how it works. I am Kind, Smart and Important, and I'd be crazy to let anyone tell me otherwise. I tried to give you a chance, several even, and I gave it my all but you kept on kicking me down. After a while I realized I wasn't going to let you tear me down to nothing. I'm human. Sure, I may not be perfect all the time, but as long as I try my hardest I deserve to be treated properly. Finally, you want to start changing once you've already pushed us all away. It's too late now. I'm sorry it had to go down like this, but I am not trash or disposable for that matter. I'm a survivor.

Sincerely,

The One That Got Away

I'm Kinda Done

Every now and then I get to these points where I'm just kinda done. Done with stress, done with attitudes, done with myself, and my insecurities, just done. I'm tired of trying to think of what other people think of me or how they see me, but at the same time I just care too much. I am truly tired. Everything within me wants to just stop caring but there's still this little part that takes me over COMPLETELY. I can't control it... yet. It drains me to think so much of the past me, present me, and future me all of which have been winging it. I fly by the seat of my pants trying to please people. I guess that's why I've never really been able to be me and I probably will never be. Just when I feel like giving up something happens where I decide I have to wing it another day. I'm realizing now I've been doing it for 19 years. Gosh, 19 years of trying to appease unappeasable people, that's tiring. I'm just so done with all the crap. When will I, and the rest of the world for that matter, just grow up and stop playing the same games over and over and over again and be mature. I guess never.

Sincerely,

The tired one

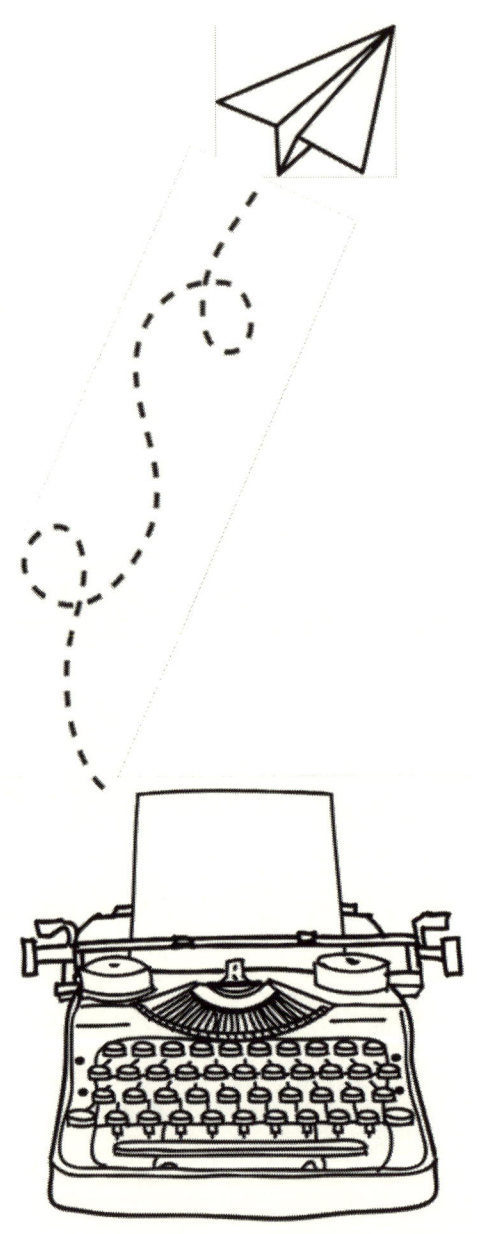

"The greatest thing you'll ever learn is to simply love and be loved in return."

~ Eden Ahbez

It's Time

It's time.

No, it's not.

Yes, it is. It's time to stop hiding behind the clothes, the hair, and whatever else you're hiding behind and just be you.

It's not that simple.

Yes, it is!

No, it's not. What if-

Uh shut up! What have you said about "what if's". It's time to move past that and just do and we will figure out what happens next together.

I can't. Even if I did we can't do this by ourselves. We're barely making it as it is. How would we make it then by ourselves?

Yes, you can! We are strong!

Shut up! I'll be more alone than I already am.

What are you talking about? There are tons of people just like you out their waiting to embrace you for who you are.

But that's not who or what I'll be coming back to when the days over. That's great and all for the moment but what about the long haul? Who will be my support team? Who'll have my back? I'll lose so many people over this.

I'm sure there will be some that still care for you and defend you through till the end.

Have you seen or heard the people around me?
That won't be happening...

True... but I still think-

You know what we need to just get on the same page.

So it's settled then.

Yep.

In unison We settle for silence, and keep to ourselves.

Here put on your "everything's fine nothing to see here" mask.

Thanks.

Applies mask

Slow Down

    Sometimes in life we get so wrapped up in the high-speed pace of life we forget to slow down and enjoy life. We're taught growing up to figure out the future without noticing the present. Life is so full of opportunities that will pass us by if we don't take the time to appreciate and seize them. Sometimes it takes going out of your way to appreciate life and if you don't you'll regret it. Look out the window. Take the long scenic drive. Be spontaneous. The best things in life are unknown and long to be discovered, that's what makes them so special. What makes these things so crucial is that they help build character. On these beaten paths is where we can discover ourselves and delve deep into self-evaluation without the input of others. You get the opportunity to see not just the world in a new light and appreciation, but yourself as well. Sure, it's easier to just zip by life not dealing with your problems or the problems around you, in which you have an impact, but it comes with a price. Things will never change, they'll only get worse. Hatred will fester, hope for change diminishes, love will slowly fade, and genuine happiness will soon be forgotten.

So seize the day in its entirety. Change for
the better the things you can. Tell your loved
ones how much they mean to you leaving out not
one detail. Compliment everyone you can. Most
importantly, slow down and enjoy life.

Push Away

I push people away in an attempt to save them. My reaction to negative things in my life is to bottle them in and bury them and put on a brave face and act like nothing's wrong. I do that so much that eventually I burst. When I explode it gets really ugly really quick. No one is safe once I've reached my limit. After months and months of bottling in my emotions, thoughts, pain, terror, and fears I finally can't handle it and I break down. It doesn't matter who you are or what you've done for me, there's no stopping the explosion once it's started. (P.S. The best thing to do when I explode is to just let it run its 5 minute coarse and not take anything I say in that short time frame personal.) I mean, I can make a grown man cry with the words that fly like sharp arrows out of my mouth in a time like this. Anytime someone's tried to "doctor" or "fix" the problem or me it just drags out the explosion time. Telling me, "It's all gonna be all right" just flames the fire and saying anything negative about me in these times could open a whole other situation that should be avoided at all costs. Months of being pulled in so many different directions, people bulling me, negativity thrown at me at a whim could all be bottled and pushed down inside of me and you, an innocent person, could do something so small but it just might be the thing that throws me overboard.

Now you may wonder "why do you feel so comfortable saying all this about yourself?" Well, because I can look in the mirror and point out my own faults and not just that of others and I'll be the first one to tell you my faults if you ask. I also want others to know why I push people away at times. It's for their own safety, not everyone could handle the flaming arrows I throw in times like this and take them with a grain of salt. Those who can recognize why what's happening is unfolding still can't always take it. I'm not proud of it but I'm not ashamed either, it's who I've been for years. I'm a work in progress and I recognize it. If you truly love someone, you don't pick and choose what parts you love and which ones you don't, you love him or her in their entirety, flaws and all. This is who I am currently, love me or don't. Just know if I'm pushing you away at a certain time it's because I'm trying to protect you.

Sincerely,

A pusher

What will make you love me?

What is it? Please, tell me! Honestly,
at this point in my life I would probably do
it. I've tried straightening my hair, wearing
name brands, I've gone thrift shopping, been
rebellious, been complacent, been strong, and
been gentle. I've recluded to the shadows, and
I've tried shining in the light, but none of
them seem to bring you to me. What is it that
you want? I've just wanted you to love me,
embrace me, and be proud of me. Most of all I've
simply wanted you to find me. In my dreams and
imagination you're right there next to me. I
can see you, feel you, hear you, sometimes even
touch you, but at the same time it seems as if
we're worlds apart. Do you or have you felt the
same way all this time. It's weird, I know but
all the best things are weird, or so I hear. I
wonder sometimes what will be the very thing that
makes you say, "Wow, I love him."

Sincerely,

Me

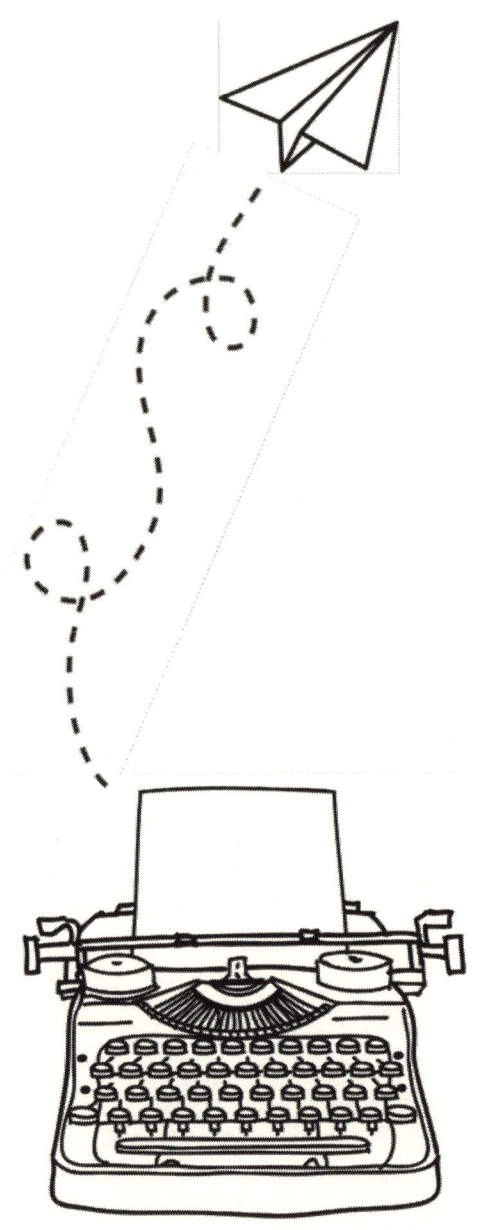

"Striving for success

Without hard work

Is like trying to harvest

Where you haven't planted"

-David Bly

Heart on a Sleeve

I wear my heart on my sleeve and I accept the blessings and the curses of doing so. To be honest it sucks sometimes but other times it's great.

Because I wear my heart on my sleeve it gives people the opportunity to break it a little easier. They play with it as if it doesn't affect the one it's connected to. They stab it, bruise it, and mangle it leaving nothing but pain and scars, but what do they care, it's not their problem to deal with. Doing this over time can cause some people's heart to grow callous and immune to emotions but that is a choice. In me it has built insecurities and each time it makes the voices of those insecurities louder and louder. Although these voices are extremely loud at times, you can't let them take control of you. If you are willing to fight then they can't control you, it's when you give in and stop fighting that they take you over. No one can make you want to fight and no one can fight for you, it's up to you.

On the other hand, wearing your heart on your sleeve allows the best friendships to build and form. Not everyone is evil or out to play

your heart. Some are here to nurture, love and
protect your heart. But you have to give them
a chance to do so and the way you do that is to
be vulnerable. Some of the people that hurt
you before were internally young and immature
(no matter how old they are externally) and you
can't always keep them at the immature state in
your mind. Allow people to grow up. You at one
point were in the same place of immaturity that
they were until you yourself grew up. You don't
want to be treated like you're a child all your
life so don't treat others the same way. Extend
mercy and give them a chance. By not letting
my past pain determine my future decisions I've
made wonderful friendships. People can say what
they want, but most of the time they're the same
people that are jealous of my life. Jealous of
the amount of people who thought I was cute or
handsome, my various adventures and vacations,
amount of friends and all the things I have or
had. They all came or happened because I allowed
myself to be vulnerable, lovable, and caring.
I've made or allowed the best friendships to
flourish because of these attributes. All these
positive things are what make me keep my heart
open and exposed on my sleeve.

Sincerely,

Heart Sleeve

Toy Heart

People treat hearts like toys.
They take what is given to them,
later tossing it to the side.
It's the ones that throw your heart so high,
you're all the way at cloud nine.
That make you forget about gravity
and its detrimental severity.
They don't want to deal with downs,
so as you fall they'll let you drown.
They're not there to catch you when you fall
but that will never stop me from loving all.

Sunrise Symphonies

Take the time to listen to the sounds that the sun bears. Wherever you are the sun is welcomed by sounds of peace and tranquility. It isn't till the rest of the world gets stirring that clamorous noise is echoed through the air.

In the woods, birds chirp their song of awakening...

At the beach, waves offer songs of forgiveness...

In the mountains, the wind offers songs of new beginnings and change…

They all have one common chorus, New Beginnings. We should start our days with a new awakening of knowledge and gratefulness to carry out through the day. We ought to be like the waves of the ocean and start our days with a new start every day . We're all offered a chance of new beginnings everyday and it's up to us to accept it. It's the ones that start their day with yesterday's chaos that bring chaos into today.

Silently,

A new day

Our life is but a vapor

Here one moment and gone the next.
Some toxic and detrimental to its environment,
some beneficial and therapeutic to exist,
their fragrance can allure or drive out,
relax or disturb.
And so we are one and the same.
We are here one moment and gone the next.
Maybe not forever in the room,
but forever we exist.

What kind of vapor are you?

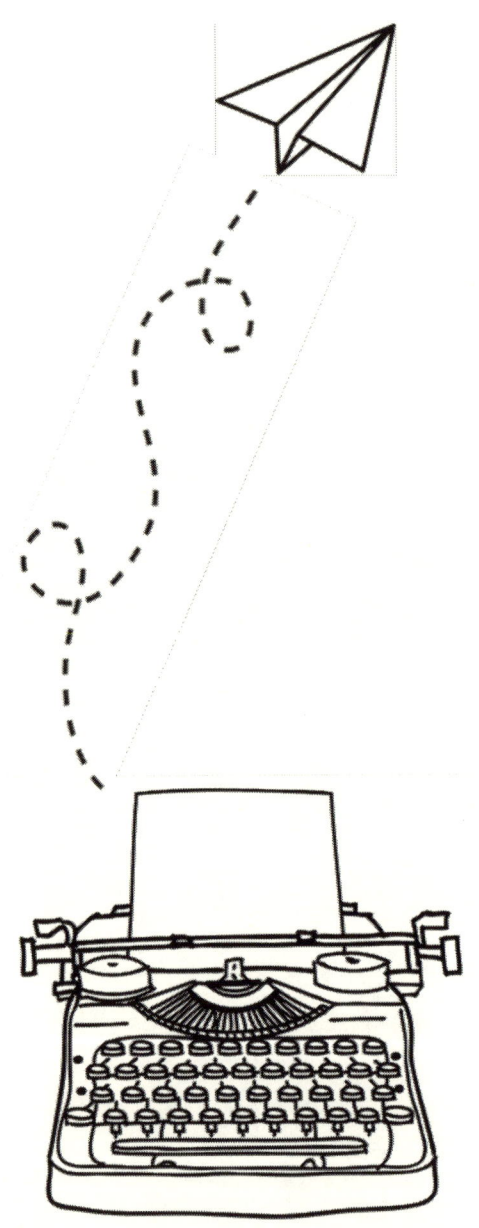

"Don't let yesterday

Take up too much of today"

~ Will Rogers

Needing Clarity

    I'm tired and fed up of dreaming and
stressing. I want to be accomplishing and
breathing. My life constantly feels like it's
buzzing without ceasing causing bouts of stress
and anxiety. I want to actually chase and
embrace the manifestation of my dreams rather
than watching them pass by when my eyes shut at
night. I want to see my goals come to fruition,
but that will only happen once action happens and
is accomplished. You don't get rewards without
work. It's hard when you don't know where to
start and no one around you does either. In this
case I must just start. Start somewhere, somehow,
but I must start NOW. If not it feels like I
might die.

Sincerely,

Action Taker

Future you

This one is to the future you. The one who stole my heart hopefully for the last time. Please don't break my heart like the last one did. I hate being compared to other people and I don't mean to do the same, but it's just a constant fear of mine. Where have you been? What took so long? I've longed to see your face and feel your embrace. I've had dreams of you before I knew you and it seemed as though you were right there. Unfortunately, when I opened my eyes you were only in my mind. I long for the day that it's not an imagination and your actually there. I hope that you're everything I hoped you be and more.

Sincerely,

Future me

Roses and Thorns

We should consider everyday as a rose. Yes, you heard me a rose. A typical standard rose in its entirety has a beautiful fragrant flower as well as a stem garnished in thorns. Some people like to act like they are one of those rose bushes that don't have thorns but we all do, those people are just in denial.

The rose flowers in our lives are all the positive things. The beautiful sunsets, delicious ice cream, that good gut-busting laugh, and anything else that's positive. These are things that make our lives beautiful, fragrant, and truly desired. Everyone has different roses and they are all beautiful. The thorns are the negative things that happen throughout the day; the plans that got cancelled, the car that didn't start, the bad news received and so on. There are typically more thorns than there are flowers but that doesn't make a rose any less desired. These thorns are things that we learn from and make us grow as individuals. I say all this to say, count your roses and your thorns and then stare and bask in the beauty of the flower and throw the thorns to the side.

Sincerely,
A rose garden

TiTi

Dreams are funny thing sometimes. They make others see you as crazy but yet at the same time it inspires others. I had this aunt who swore 'til the day she passed that she was going to be a superstar. Not a day goes by that she didn't confess her dream and speak it into the atmosphere. She would tell anybody and everybody that would listen, because she had her heart set on the fact that she was going to be a superstar and boy you couldn't tell her any different. Whenever I told her about my dreams or things that I was doing she would tell me, "Don't forget me when you get famous" and "You better take me with you when you get famous." She always told me no matter what I was doing and even when I wasn't doing anything at all that, "One day, you believe me now, you're gonna be a star and don't let anyone tell you differently." I always kind of brushed it off like "okay, sure". However, If you think about it she truly was onto something. You've got to know who you are. Regardless of the circumstance and situations life throws at you, you've got to chase your dreams. She didn't care if she was just the superstar of her house; at the end of the day she was a superstar. If she touched no one else's heart in this whole world, she touched mine.

Sincerely,
Titi's Superstar

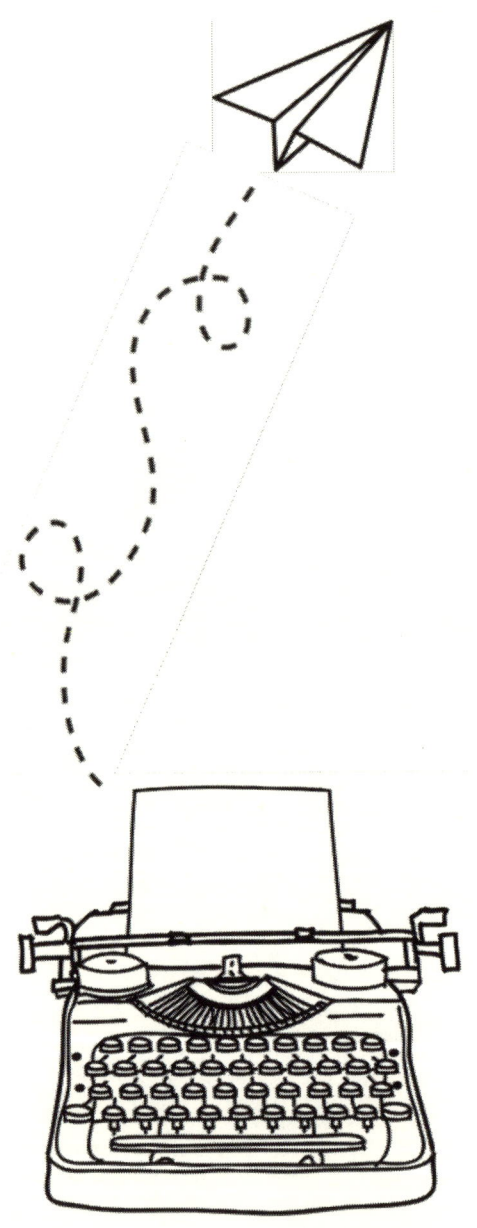

"Promote what you love

Don't bash what you hate"

- Lilly Singh

<u>Trees</u>

One of my favorite quotes in life is one I heard while watching one of my favorite Tyler Perry movies. He made the analogy of people to trees. He puts everyone in his life through the "Tree Test". It goes like this:

LEAF PEOPLE:
Some people come into your life and they are like leaves on a tree. They are only there for a season. You can't depend on them or count on them because they are weak and only there to give you shade. Like leaves, they are there to take what they need and as soon as it gets cold or a wind blows in your life they are gone. You can't be angry at them, it's just who they are.

BRANCH PEOPLE:
There are some people who come into your life and they are like branches on a tree. They are stronger than leaves, but you have to be careful with them. They will stick around through most seasons, but if you go through a storm or two in your life it's possible that you could lose them. Most times they break away when it's tough. Although they are stronger than leaves, you have to test them out before you run out there and

100

*put all your weight on them. In most cases they
can't handle too much weight. But again, you
can't be mad with them, it's just who they are.*

ROOT PEOPLE:
*If you can find some people in your life who are
like the roots of a tree then you have found
something special. Like the roots of a tree,
they are hard to find because they are not trying
to be seen. Their only job is to hold you up and
help you live a strong and healthy life. If you
thrive, they are happy. They stay low key and
don't let the world know that they are there.
And if you go through an awful storm they will
hold you up. Their job is to hold you up, come
what may, and to nourish you, feed you and water
you.*

*Just as a tree has many limbs and many leaves,
there are few roots. Look at your own life. How
many leaves, branches and roots do you have?
What are you in other people's lives?*

Ever since I heard this, I have tried to do
the same thing. I believe this to be very true
and more importantly powerful. So ask yourself
what kind of person am I in other peoples lives?

Sincerely,

A Tree

It's Me

Why do people always hate me?
Is it the way I look,
the way I dress,
the way I speak,
or the way I see?

What did I ever do to you?
I tried my best,
I did what you wanted,
when you wanted,
I only loved you in return.

Did I say something?
I thought I spoke love,
spoke joy, spoke like you.
Was it not what you wanted?
I guess I'm just a thing to you.

Can you really just throw me away like a thing?
I'm fading just like you
but maybe you'll just last longer.
Just know, the scars they still hurt
but after all, I'm just a thing.

Was it really all me?

It's my fault this happened.

It seems I'm the only one who's suffering.

I need to leave you alone.

As you can see it always comes back to me.

The Mask

A child struggled in his ways; ways that
no one could help. He tried his best, but that
wasn't enough. He sought approval from those
here below; always forgetting whom he really
impressed on High. Stressed in school, looking
for help: only to find a fleeting hope at best. He
longed for more than what was before him. "Reach
for the star," they told him, as they smacked
his hands down. "Go for the gold," they said as
he tripped and stumbled by their actions. His
best was never good enough; his generosity was
spit upon. "I'm trying my best," he said while
down on his knees. They spoke in disgust. They
yelled in his face, "You don't even try," was the
refrain. Tears stained his face. Heart beaten,
bruised, aching, scared from the constant turmoil
he felt inside. He put on a mask and pushed on
through. Days go by. Moods change. Yet behind
the mask his tears still remain.

Sincerely,

The boy behind the mask

The City of Me

I've spent so many years of my life keeping all my social circles separate. Think of it like a city.

THE GHETTO:

These people know me to be all kinds of "ghetto" and hood-tastic. I come from the DMV, but more importantly Hoodbridge. I know every new dance, song, and celebrity hot topic there is to know.

THE HIPSTER:

These people know me for being all kinds of aesthetic. From my music choices, to fashion sense, to language, meals, and style I sweat hipster but, without all the weed and drugs. But seriously I drive with my windows down blaring that new indie track, while wearing my thrift shop clothes while on my way to a small hidden coffee shop with these people.

THE CITY:

These people know me for being prim and proper. I'm a perfect addition to society and in every manner to them. I never leave the house without looking completely put together. I only wear name brand and I must always be on top of the latest trends and fashions for this season.

THE FAMILY/CHURCH:

These people for the most part know me as the little boy who grew up in church and only some know about my "dark times". But for the most part I've kept a relatively normal appearance to these people. I tend to be more chill and relaxed around them because it seems like a safe haven.

The one thing all these groups have in common, besides my addiction to clothes and their importance to me, is none of these groups truly know all of me. One group may know more about me in one area than another and vice versa. I've also kept walls up between these different groups of people so no one would intermix and share what they knew about me with each other. It was my way of controlling people and what they knew about me but after all these years those walls have come down. Everybody gets to know everything. The whole "City of Me" will get to know each other and whatever happens will happen.

Sincerely,

Mayor Me

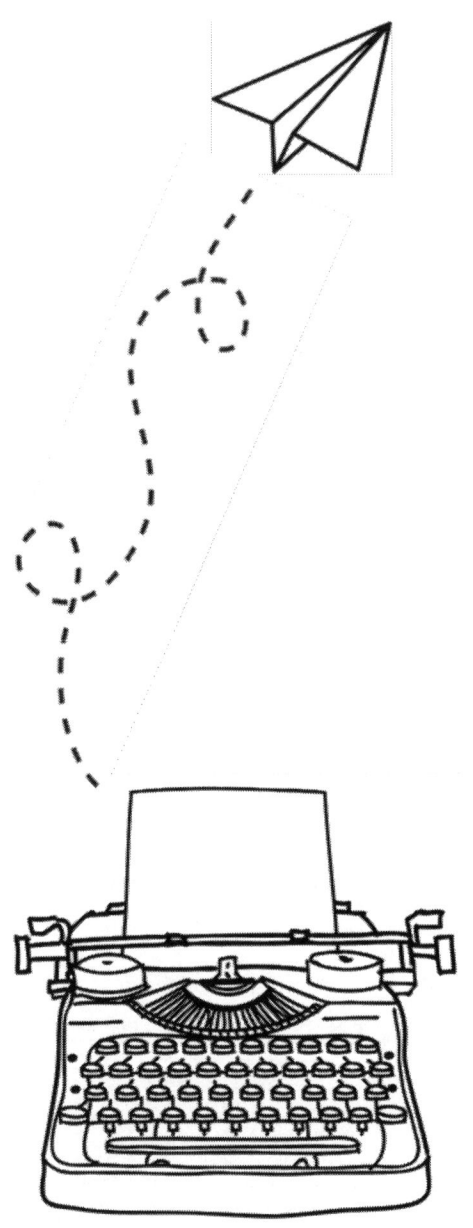

"Don't trust everything you see.

Even salt looks like sugar."

~ Anonymous

Overflow

A good friend of mine once taught me a really good lesson about pouring into other people. People are going to want you to pour into them and your going to want to pour into other people. That's okay but we need to be aware of the way in which we pour into other people. We should never tip our cup to pour into other people, because after constantly tipping and pouring out our cup we will end up empty. The proper way in which to pour into other people is to stay upright and let God fill us. When we let God constantly pour into and fill us eventually begin to overflow. It's that overflow that people should be filled from. If we ourselves are overflowing then that means we won't run empty because we are staying upright. God said that he would fill us to the overflow but we have to let him do so in the first place.

Sincerely,

An Upright Cup

Wishbone vs. Backbone

Something that you need to remember is to not let a wishbone grow where a backbone belongs. You can't go through life just wishing that things will happen or will change. You yourself need to take the initiative to make them change. If a car is speeding at you I'm not just going to think and wish to myself that you'd move out the way, I scream, "Get out the way." If you still don't move I will then go and push you out the way. TAKE INITIATIVE. If you want to stand around wishing and hoping for things to change without taking action then please find a quiet corner out of the way of the people that are taking action and SHUT UP.

If you're tired of being treated like trash, less then, worthless, and like your opinion doesn't matter than speak up. You bottling it all in and then popping off at other people and running your little mouth is only going to get you in trouble.

Don't let people push you around or treat other people any old way. Stand up. Say something. You were given a voice for a reason so use it. We weren't made to follow just any person that waltzed up in our lives. We were

only made to follow Christ. Grow a backbone
for heavens sake and stop being scared. Man
up. Woman up. Be strong, independent, and stop
letting other people determine who you are and
how you're going to treat your friends, family,
and whoever else. If they want to be rude and
nasty to people then let them, that doesn't mean
you have to do it too.

Genuinely,

A Backbone

Where you at

I'm writing this letter to make sure you're okay. I didn't see you at church this Sunday and this ain't the first time either. Don't get to thinkin' now that its okay to just miss church whenever you feel like it. God ain't here to convenience you. I think you misunderstood the Pastor when they said, "He's our Buckler" He didn't say, "butler". He ain't your personal servant, here to wait on your hand and foot. You're supposed to be seeking His face, asking Him what He wants you to do not the other way around. You can't tell God, "I can't do this whole go to church thing today", I'm tired and got a headache", then an hour later you're in your warm bed under the covers crying to the Lord, "Oh Lord, please deliver me from this headache, by your stripes I am healed form the top of my head to soles of my feet." Let out a loud "HALLELUJAH" and a soft "in Jesus name, amen" in a whole overly dramatic voice and expect some grand miracle delivering you from your headache. That ain't how this works. Maybe, just maybe, you wouldn't have that headache if your tail was in church. I bet you didn't think I heard about what happened the night before, hmm.

It ain't the devil makin' you tired and giving you that headache. It was the fact that you were up all late the night before doin' whatever you were doin'. It ain't my business. Also, stop sending me all these text messages an hour or so before church talkin' 'bout why you won't be there this Sunday. You're getting a little bit too predictable. Just know all them kids you had ain't no viable excuse for your absences. Your kids ain't preventing you from getting to church on time. Admit it you just didn't want to come. Anyways, love you. Hopefully I'll see you at church and if not I'll probably see you afterwards at the family event (even though you said you were to sick to make it to church). Anyways, God bless!

Sincerely,

Your fellow church member

The Sun Above the Clouds

   Have you ever thought about the way the sun is above the clouds in a deep profound way? The sun is completely and totally unapologetic. It spreads it rays without the hindrances of barriers. Even on the cloudiest day, above the clouds the sun still is spreading its rays relentlessly. The clouds amplify the unseen beauty of the sun giving it dimension and complexity. The remembrance of its beauty draws me to the sky longing for another glimpse. It seems almost ... addicting in a way. I could stare at the sky for hours without moving, longing for another taste. The sky blesses me with beautiful arrays of color, beauty, dimension but none the same as the kind that lies only above the clouds. Sure, sunsets and sunrises enchant me but just like many things in life they are only temporal. If I were above the clouds I could stare at the beauty as long as my plane could fly. That's where the problem lies though. We have to be willing to fly above the clouds in order to see the absolute beauty the sky posses. We must take the courage and the strength to fly above the clouds and storms of life, because above them we finally realize a reason to keep flying.

Sincerely,
Someone in the clouds

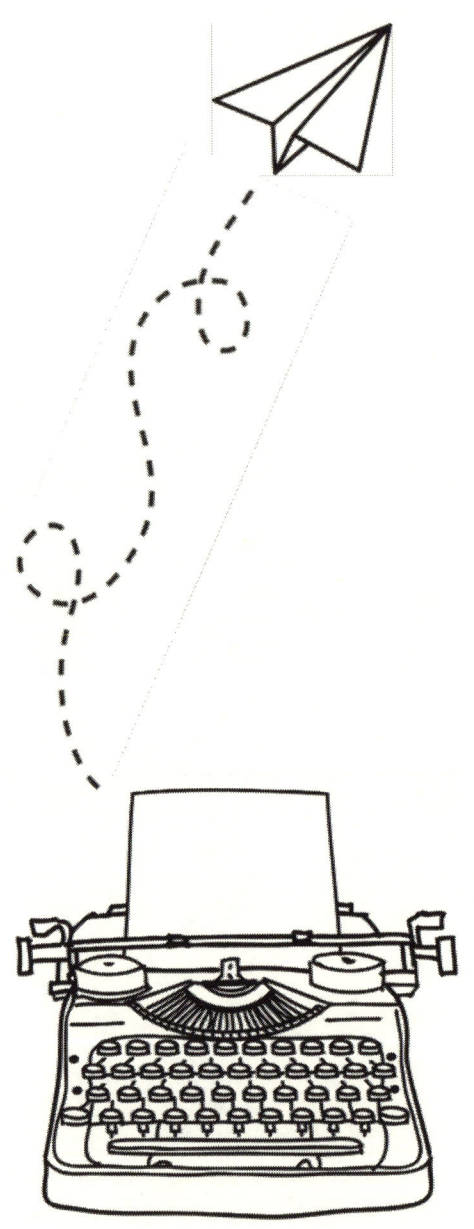

"I don't know where I'm going from here

but I promise it won't be boring"

~ David Bowie

Set me Free

I stand on the shore, scared of the waters ahead.
You beckon me to board the ship of my heart.
I board in terror,
you promise of freedom.

I shake at the sight of the fog on the water.
You stay steadfast, taking me for where I am.
I realize you were the One Trustworthy.
You sing Freedom.

You ravish me, daring me to seize the sea.
I let out the sails of my heart.
Your face streams with tears.
I beckon freedom.

You run to me grasping me tight.
I fall in your arms, overwhelmed in love.
You look me in my eyes.
I plead "Oh, Lord set me free".

Nataph

Years have past and our land is dry.
The season of testing is upon us.
We've heard the promises of the rain.
But many have begun to forget Your power.
Doubt has swept the land and choked hope,
causing the many to turn from You.
But I still have seed in the ground.

There are still a select few of us who believe.
We have abandoned our hope in earth
and we look earnestly to the Sky.
We hear the sound of thunder on the horizon
and feel the Nataph run down our face.
The many think we're crazy
but we have seed in the ground.

Us few cry to the Sky for the rain.
You reply with a loud thundering "Receive".
We open our eyes to see rain approaching,
water from the Sky floods our land.

And the many find it to be a pest

but we are busy filling our vessels and praising
our Lord.

Because Rain only matters to Those who have seed
in the ground.

Yes & Amen

I will say what He says
as I walk in His ways,
as I walk in the light.
He's making it all right.
I put down my thoughts & feelings
which keeps me rocking and reeling.
Saying Yes & Amen,
My God has a plan.

It's a plan for my good.
All things working as it should.
Staying holy & pure tstio Him,
Not moving by a whim.
Saying Yes & Amen,
My God has a plan.

I will judge Him by His promises alone,
not by things that are going on.
While I say what He says,
As I keep walking in the way,
His promises are sure.
To all who endure,
saying Yes & Amen,
For my God has a plan.

No more doubt here.

I have no place for fear.

Staying strong then I'll see,

He's bringing it all to pass for me.

Saying Yes & Amen,

My God has a plan.

<u>Stop, Listen, Learn</u>

Today while getting ready to leave for the airport I felt compelled to "stop, listen, and learn". I bought two new necklaces on this trip and already owned one and with these three I found a deeper meaning than just 3 pieces of jewelry. I saw what I aspire to do:

<u>The Metal Plates:</u>

Remind me to write my own story. Don't let other people or circumstances dictate who I am or who I want to be. Currently they are smooth but as time goes on they will get rough, they'll get scratches, and they won't be as pretty and shiny. It's just like us we start off shiny, bright and reflect what we see and are taught. But as time goes on we get scratches, bruises, and scars but they tell our story and remind us of lessons we've learned. It shows that we've lived, and that's what I want, I WANT TO LIVE LIFE TO THE FULLEST. I'll accept the scars and I'll tell the stories and I'll share the lessons I've learned and in the end it shows I LIVE LIFE AND I CONQUER IT!

<u>The Gold Tooth:</u>

Don't stop fighting. Even when others give up... I MUST persevere, push on and push past obstacles and circumstances. DON'T STOP, DON'T

GIVE IN, FIGHT. It reminds me of the tooth worn by Native Americans or even Africans of the beast they had slain. It encourages me by reminding me of all the giants, all the circumstances, and all the trials that tried to break me down but only made me stronger. It reminds me that I AM STRONG, I CAN WIN, I WON'T GIVE UP. I AM WARRIOR.

The Cross:

Everything has to be done with Christ. All actions should and must be done with the right godly intentions and motives. If things aren't done with God, IT WILL FAIL. If we would do everything in sync and in unison with God it would make things a lot easier, and we'd be happier people. No one not even God said it would be easy that's why He gave us 1) The Comforter 2) Himself and 3) The ability to have a relationship with him. That way when we fail, He will pick us back up so that we can push on. He wants to help us, we just have to let him. The Cross reminds me to LOVE without limitations, without boarders, without end. There should never be a point in our lives where we stop loving ANYONE. We are supposed to forgive, forget and love. It's not hard but it's not always easy. We were created to love and be loved and when we allow pain to enter us and take place in us it prevents us from doing the very thing we were created to do.... love.

Sincerely,
Inspired One

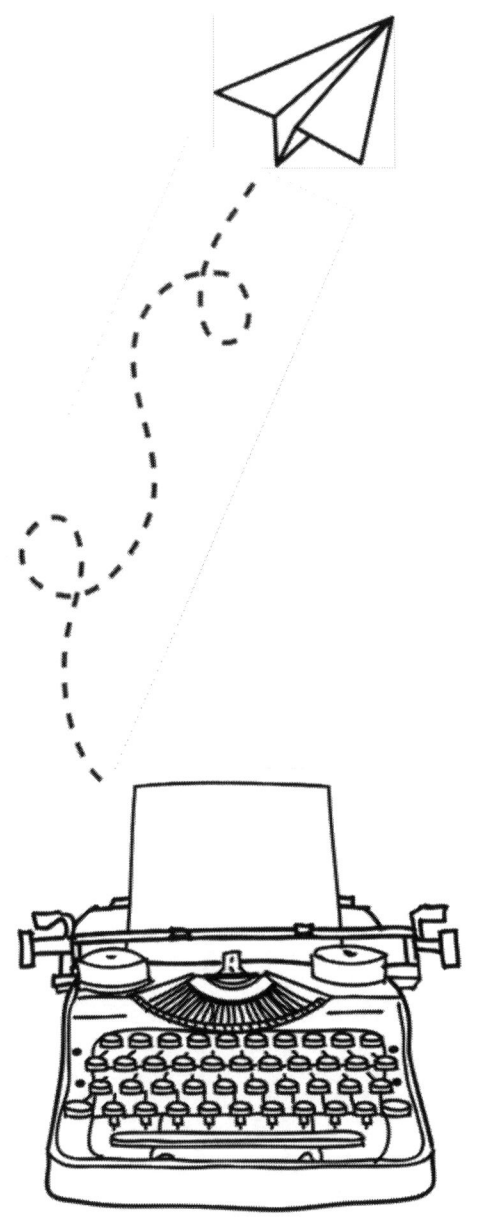

"Honey, folks are gonna talk

About you 'til the day you die,

And ain't nothing you can do.

LET FOLKS TALK!

It ain't about what they call

you.

It's what you answer to."

~ Madea (Tyler Perry)

If No one Loves You?

I was once asked, "So, if no one loves you, then what?" I didn't think much of it for a while until finally I had a revelation. I had been looking at the question wrong the entire time. I was so busy trying to figure out what would happen to me if no one loved me that I almost missed a revelation that I so desperately needed at the time.

No matter if no one in the world loved me, I still need to love everyone in the world. Whoa! Let's take that a little deeper. Even if everyone in the world curses my name and tries to kill me, I still love them. Maybe, you're still not getting it? No matter what you do or say to me, I'm still going to love you. What the what is the what the what? Right about now you think I'm crazy, I know but let me explain. Christ commands us to love everyone. It's of the upmost importance to him that we love. Christ is not like man He leads by example.

Christ saw us all in the moments of His capture, His beating and even His crucifixion and never once did He regret dying for us. He knew that the men beating Him needed a Savior and He loved them just the same. He knew what

I was gonna go through so He sacrificed himself just for me. Look at yourself. He knew you... let that sink in. Christ knew you and what you were going to go through and knew that His death was the only way you were gonna make it. Let me put it this way. He physically died to prove to them, to me, to you that there is nothing He wouldn't do for us. Christ suffered more than any of us will so that you wouldn't have to deal with drugs, alcohol, abuse, depression, suicide, anxiety and whatever else. Just think all He asked you to do is forgive and love everyone. Not just your friends, your family, and your co-worker, all of which we still can't do, but even go so far as to love our enemies.

Sincerely,

Someone trying to love

Defend Me

You say that you were "always on my side" but it seems like that is nothing but a lie. You say, "I've always defended you," but never did. Every time someone does something negative to me and I dare speak out, you immediately tell me I'm over-reacting or am taking it the wrong way. You make it seem that no one is wrong when they mistreat me; everyone is justified and had the right to do so. It's always my fault, but not my fault. Make up your mind! You think your some kind of stable person in my life but every five-seconds you change and are never in my favor. You vacation with those that burned me constantly growing up. You defend them and treat them like gold and leave me to keep your guys' world revolving and expect me to put mine on hold to do so.

I tell you what's stressing me; you listen, and then do nothing. You say that your gonna do something but never follow through. You can deny it all but it's true. If you want me to believe something different then give me something else to believe. You defend my demons and trick my trust. I've been telling you "Someday, these people are gonna learn. I don't care if I have to

break down every ounce of their ego to do so, but
they will learn. They will not treat me however
they want." Well, guess what? You're not
exempt. I gave you a taste test, forgave you,
and since you want to keep on playing it's time
for you to sit down and take the whole plate.
Fool me once, shame on you. Fool me twice can't
put the blame on you. But don't worry there
won't be a "twice" someone's gonna learn a lesson
here.

Bon Appetite,

Your chef

Leave me alone

You make your den in thieves,
and bury your heart in thorns.
Don't fly away like leaves
and come again in May.
Don't break my heart just to see
my heart constantly mourn.
Your desire is to make my heart grieve.
Why won't you leave my alone?

Regret

Maybe I should have,

and then again maybe I shouldn't have.

You only really know once it's too late.

To take it all back I would give anything.

Had I only shut my mouth, would I be any happier?

It's these very thoughts that constantly swarm my
mind.

Regret is what I see when I look back.

Trying desperately to undo the damage done

even though I know it's impossible.

Everyday saying, "Today I'll undo the damage",

never realizing I just dig my hole deeper.

Tears become tattoos.

Heart remains too raw to beat for another.

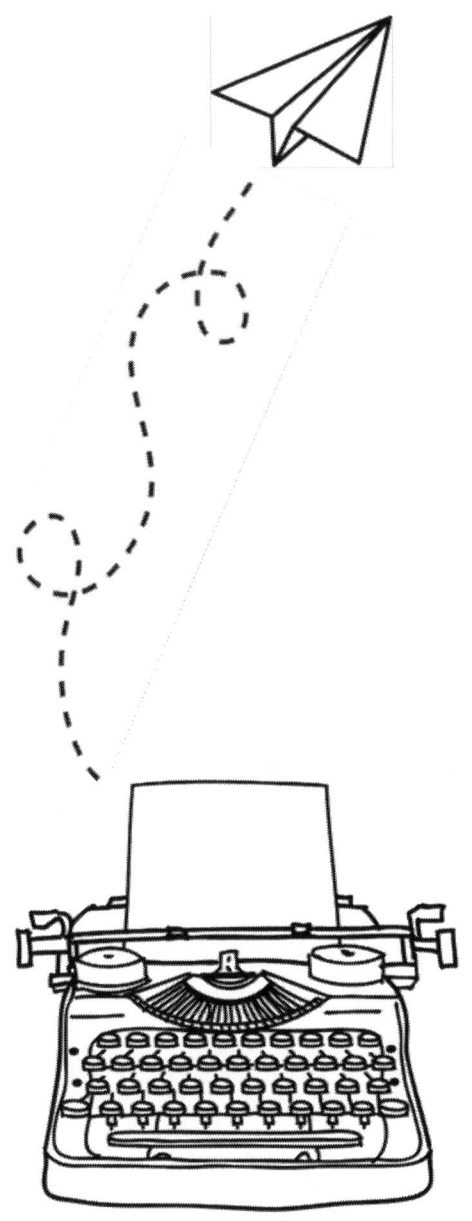

Das Leben ist schön

(life is beautiful)

~ Anonymous

Since When

Since when did you let what other people
do determine who you are? Since when do you let
people run over you? Stand up and fight! You let
the circumstances that were around you determine
who you were going to be. If everybody was going
to be hateful you were just going to let them
turn you to hate? Everybody else hates this
person so are you gonna hate that person too? If
someone tells you "don't like that person, don't
love that person, don't help them," are you just
gonna listen or are you going to go and make your
own assessment? It doesn't matter how anyone
else feels, you have to make up in your mind who
you are going to be. It doesn't matter if the
entire world calls you crazy because maybe, just
maybe, you're the sane one and everyone else is
crazy. Don't let other peoples "High and Mighty"
attitude turn your character sour. You are not
the judge, jury and executioner. You are a
servant not a master. You don't get to determine
everyone else's fate, no matter who you think you
are. No one gave you permission to start your
own mission of being "The Grand Judge". No one
gave you the power to determine if someone should
live or die; so don't go assuming it. You need
to be worried about only yourself (in a humble
way) before you start running and getting in
everyone else's business.

Sincerely,
A People Pleaser

In Your Corner

I'm in your corner don't you see? All the time you've been in the ring I was there for you, with you, and rooting for you. All the teachings that you learned throughout life while in My house were prepping you for this very moment. You scream and cry when the devil knocks you down, "God where are you?" I'm right here, get up! Fight until you can't fight anymore. Give it your all! Take back everything the devil stole. He's not going to just hand it over to you, you're going to have to fight. Don't you want your happiness and joy, peace and sleep, ambition and drive back? What about your friends and family are you ready and willing to give them all over to him? If not then fight! Take back the drug addicts, the prostitutes, the alcoholics, the broken hearted, the victims, the abandoned, the depressed and the oppressed. The raped and molested, the manipulated and the manipulators go get them all! Don't give up, don't settle, don't just lay there, GET UP! The devil isn't going to stop once he's stolen everything, he's not going to stop once he's knocked you down, he's going to keep on going until you die. SO get up, fight, and you show him who's the boss around here. Believe in the power of Us, and you show him what for. It's time to stop playing in the ring and get things done. Let's finish this once and for all.

Honestly,
THE COACH

Living Lesson

Never forget the end goal.
The taking back what the enemy stole,
The restoration of tattered souls.

Aspire to the high calling of the Father,
loving without penalties or a soul barter.
Leaving my pain where I became a starter.

Never let your age define you,
mind contain you,
Or hope on the horizon tire you.

Notice the beauty in life
and forgive strife,
only then will you begin to enjoy life.

Yes you can, don't start to lack,
I've got your back.
I love you to the moon and back.

In Season & Out

There is a season to mourn
for the breaking of a heart,
for the stealing of a soul
and for a loss of a harvest.

There is a season to laugh
for the jokes that fill our hearts,
for the sun and its fun,
for the dancing in the rain.

There is a season of tears
for the new life that has begun,
for the life that has moved on,
for the words that can't be undone.

There is a season of sowing
for the feast that's yet to come,
for the work that must be done,
for the blessings soon to come.

There is a season of rain
for the washing away,
for the springing forth of new life
and for the cooling of the heat.

There is a season of rest
from the work that has been done,
from the battles that we faced,
from the stress of our test,

There is a season of harvest
for the work that we put in,
for the filling of our stomach
and for the encouragement of our souls.

No Better Season

No one season is more important than another. I'm grateful for the season I'm in no matter what it is, because no matter how bad it may be the season will eventually change. When a season is hard I try to remember the good that lies on the other side. When a season is good I ravish in it, enjoying all it has to offer. Understanding that there are seasons helps me better understand that there is much more to life then just me and what I'm going through. Even though I may be in a good season I have to remember that someone else may be in a bad one. Granted that isn't gonna make me not enjoy mine. But rather it makes me more grateful for where I'm at in life, while still being able to lend a helping hand to others in need. Some seasons are hot and intense and some are cool and delightful but at the end of the day it's all part of life. Seasons, if you take full advantage of them, keep you from getting complacent in life. If all we had were good times all the time we would never realize how good we have it. If we only had harsh and rather hard seasons we would altogether give up on life. It is important to recognize and learn from the seasons we are in.

Sincerely,
Someone enjoying a season

May, June, July

May started pains
through loose lips
by open doors
and with fake joy.

June brought pain
through false hope,
by straining friendships
and with a sudden fall.

July killed confidence
through a weak heart
by ignoring the signs
and with a "you come on too strong".

Reach, Press, Believe

Boom...

The doors have opened

and our desires (freedom/answers/hope) are available.

Reach, press, believe the time is now.

Boom... Snap!

The sifter is broken

and he who works it flees

and you are set free.

Reach, press, believe the time is now and you are the one!

Boom... Snap!... Clink...

The chains are broken

and the captive set free.

Future generations now have a fighting chance.

It only took the one to...

Reach, press, believe the time is now and you are the one to who power is given.

Memories

Childhood memories are starting to spoil.
Waves once jumped are now crashing.
The walls were bursting with people and love
but the growing population has now grown scarce.
Desires to stay are now desires to leave,
and now it's just me, my thoughts, and the sea.

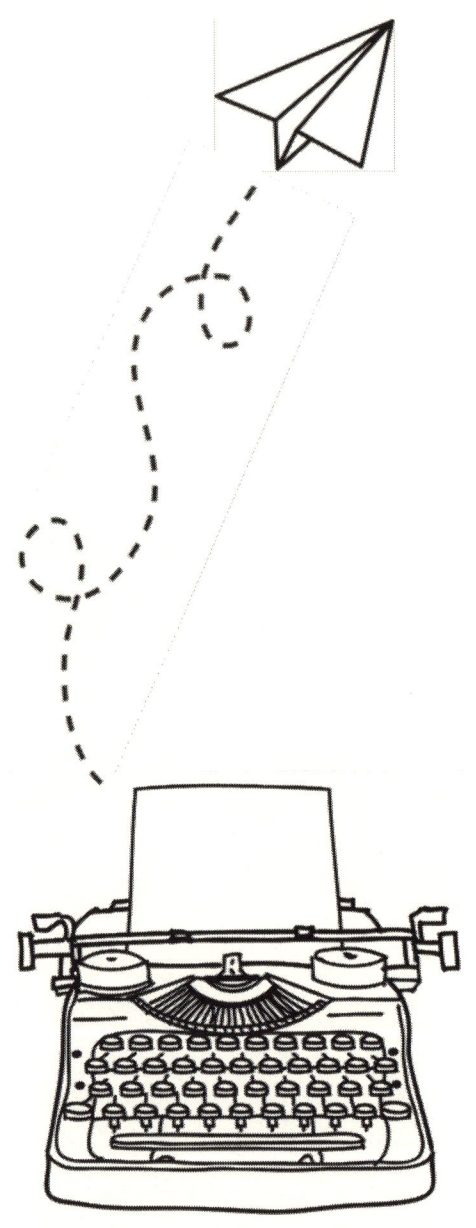

"Shine your Light!"

~ My Buddy

Whistle Turtle

Whistle Turtle,

Whistle Turtle,

Sing your song.

Whistle Turtle,

Whistle Turtle,

The War has begun.

Whistle Turtle,

Whistle Turtle,

Keep marching on.

Tired

Here I find myself once again tired,
drained, empty, lonely, but more importantly
broken. Broken from disappointment. Broken from
missed chances. Just simply broken. Everyday
seems like it could be my last and every breath
could be taken. I know it doesn't seem like
this is how I feel but deep down it is. I try
to hide my pain but sometimes it just seeps out.
I continue to push pretending to not feel this
way hoping I'll convince myself but nevertheless
here I return with tattered heart. A million
vacations and therapy sessions isn't gonna fix me.
Someone preaching at me relentlessly isn't gonna
fix me either. I can't explain it, but if I had
to its that I'm just simply tired.

Sincerely,

A tired soul

Can't stop, won't stop

Everyday I wonder if I'll make it through another day again. My legs don't feel like supporting me and my heart just isn't there. I feel like passing out and falling asleep but I know in my heart I have to press on. I guess that's why they said there's a fighter in me. No matter how bad I want to give up, I won't. I push, I fight, and I grind only to repeat it again. I fight just to fight and I always win. Sure I would like to rest but it just never seems to happen with me. From the moment I open my eyes till the moment I close them I don't stop grinding. The hustles don't stop and they won't stop. Even though I can't always see my reward all the time, it's coming just you wait and see.

Sincerely,

A hustler

<u>Striving to hold onto</u>
<u>happiness</u>

     In this very moment I want to cry.
Maybe it's the drama of life, maybe it's the
opportunities that pass by. Regardless, at
the end of each day there's still this weird
sad, broken and empty feeling. There are small
moments of utter peace and enjoyment but sadly,
they last only a mere minute if that. I strive
to hold onto those moments and ravish in them but
alas they still pass by like the seconds on a
clock. When you think about it how do you hold
onto something that is intangible like happiness
or time? A life filled with few highs, many
grinds at a break even level, and just as many
lows is not a pleasant life to live. Sadly,
it's the life that's been given to me; but that
doesn't mean I have to accept it right?

Sincerely,

Happy Time Holder

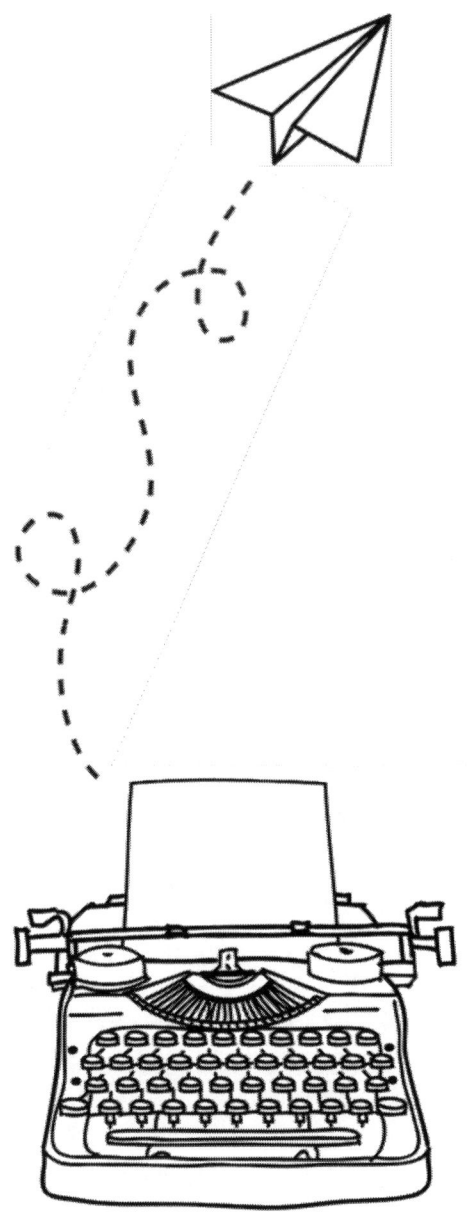

"Stand up for what you believe in,

Even if it means standing alone."

~ Anonymous

A Large Place

I'll meet you in the stillness. I've walked on water, I've walked through the desert, I've walked where no one else has ever glimpsed. I created you so I can see you, love you, and meet you. Just to be in your presence making a connection is a blessing to Me. I created a large place for you and Me to commune in peace. No one can touch us here. They see only from afar but never able to come near. No matter how rough the storm, we will remain steadfast here in the stillness of our "Large Place". You, Oh you, I especially delight to be with. There is no time with us and there is no stopping us. You can come and go as you please, you are not My prisoner but rather My child but I will always be right here in the stillness of our "Large Place".

Sincerely,

ABBA

White Picket Fence

What lies beyond (outside) the white picket
fence?

Is it the picture perfect lover,

and straight "A' Harvard bound child,

maybe an obedient pet.

All with full stomachs, closets, and bank
accounts,

all the latest little gadgets,

and not a struggle in sight,

Is it all you ever wanted? Is it what you
expected?

Is it what you thought?

What lies beyond (Inside) the white picket fence?

Is it the abusive blind love,

and the strung out kid,

maybe a couple bullet holes.

All starving, broke, and with one outfit,

all the latest drugs,

and no future in sight.

Is it all you ever wanted? Is it what you
expected?   Is it what you thought?

Same outside,

Different inside.

Both struggle,

some just don't show it.

Four Walls

A person caged inside the four walls of someone's control with what seems like no escape has crowded my space. The walls never provide them with more room no matter how old they get. The walls will grow taller and their will to fight only grows skewed. They try to escape looking and hoping to find a way out or over but none are seen. Somehow I've found myself locked and trapped inside someone else's walls of problems, or should I say someone else's personal dungeon. I have my own hurdles to deal with and the walls they have trapped me in are walls that I've already dealt with and conquered. I'm in a different season in life, but because this person desires my progress they cling to me desperately. The problem is that just because I have progressed in this particular situation does not mean the other person also immediately progresses as well. One person's progress is not always everyone's progress. Personal happiness in ones life is gained by their own fights, trials, and victories. I can help you but I can't fight for you. If you are unhappy you have to make up in your mind to either change the way things are and deal with the repercussions thereof, or shut up and deal with it. Don't go complaining to everyone about your problems that only you can change. It's up to you to break your walls.

Butterfly Lungs

There's something about somebody else admiring your work, especially something that you're so passionate about. For instance, it was the forth of July and one of our family friends was telling me how much an ongoing project I was working so hard on moved her. It gave me the strength to keep on pushing and striving to achieve my goals. For me, when someone I'm not closely related to loves and boast about a project I'm working on it makes me feel like it's all worth it. Sure, when family says something positive I appreciate it but when it comes from somebody else who doesn't really know me or my story it hits me a little deeper. Just to know that the sleepless nights, the pouring out of my heart, the relentless dedication all helped someone makes it all worth it. Appreciation from repetition can be said to anyone about anything frivolously but appreciation from the heart has depth, dimension, love, and sincerity behind it that gives it meaning to the recipient. The best way to explain the feeling is, it's like a couple little butterflies are fluttering in my lungs. In my mind the little butterflies have blue wings, but yours can be whatever color you want.

Sincerely,

Butterfly Lungs

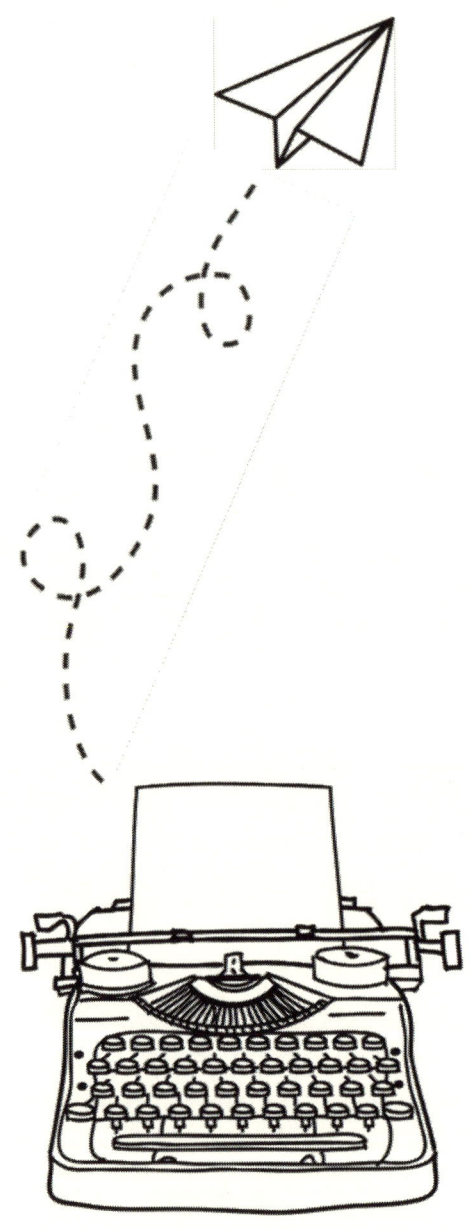

"If you cannot let go

You yourself will never go..."

~ Old Soul

I Give Roses

I give a rose to those I love.
To those I will,
to those I trust.

To give a rose is to give my heart.
To give my life,
to give my story.

A rose is beautiful but protected.
To keep itself safe,
to keep itself strong.

At one time or another the bush may die.
But to remember my time I keep a rose to dry,
so when my time is up you can keep my time alive.

Falling Apart

My tired hands don't work the same. My broken spirit doesn't feel the same. My weary mind feels old and tired. My heart remains hurt and broken but open ripe for another beating. How is it that my heart has broken in so many different ways by so many different people? Never have my lips touched another's, and never has another kept my heart and still I've fallen out of love and crashed like everyone else. They say you have to love yourself first but how can you do that when you're not even sure that your worthy of love or that someone would even want to love you. Every glimpse of romance leaves me believing that something is wrong with me. So how do you love yourself when all your negative features are the only reflection in mirror? I guess I never really gave my heart a chance to heal, or maybe it was never in one piece to begin with but either way I don't remember what it feels like to be whole. How many cries for help will have to echo in the breeze, hit hollow ears, and be ignored before I give up? Will I be able to bounce back forever or will I be knocked down one day and not be able to get back up? I already see my body's not bouncing back as fast as it used to. "Its too early", I cry, "I need more time." Slowly though the cries get softer and softer.

Sincerely,
A Single Soul

I let Go

I let go of my pride first and foremost. All my doubt and unbelief I cast out. I let myself go and hold myself to a higher standard of living. I will try to not hold my past against me but rather encourage myself to grow as a person and learn from my mistakes and pain. I forgive any and all transgressions done against me. Those that hurt me, scared me, and broke me I release you. Every family member close and distant that hurt me, I let you go. Every toxic friendship I forgive. Every teacher who gave up on me, I bless you. I will not cast you physically out of my life but rather I hold no aught against you. I will not hold anyone to an impossible standard they cannot achieve, rather take them for where they are and love them regardless. I wish the best for you, and I understand that what I want you to do may not be the ultimate plan for your life. Death is not a thing I bestow upon anyone, not even those I'm not fond of. I hate no one because I understand the true meaning behind the word hate. By holding onto all past transgressions against me I hold back myself from progressing personally in any way. Forgiveness is the key and I hold the power to use it to set love and happiness free in my own life. To hold onto animosity and expect peace is to be ignorant.

Sincerely,

Myself

Stories Untold

Stories untold are lives untouched.
They are the problems unsolved
and they are the wisdom with held.

They could be the key to someone's future
maybe the very words they needed to heal.
There is strength behind every story.

From them strength is drawn,
from them a new perspective has dawned,
from them the next generation goes in.

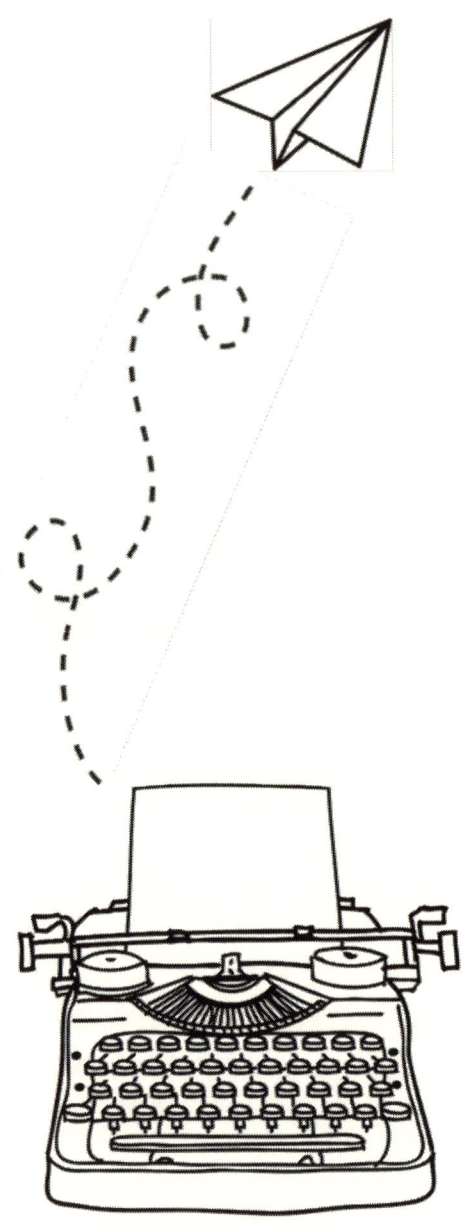

"We accept the love

We think we deserve"

~ Perks of Being a Wallflower

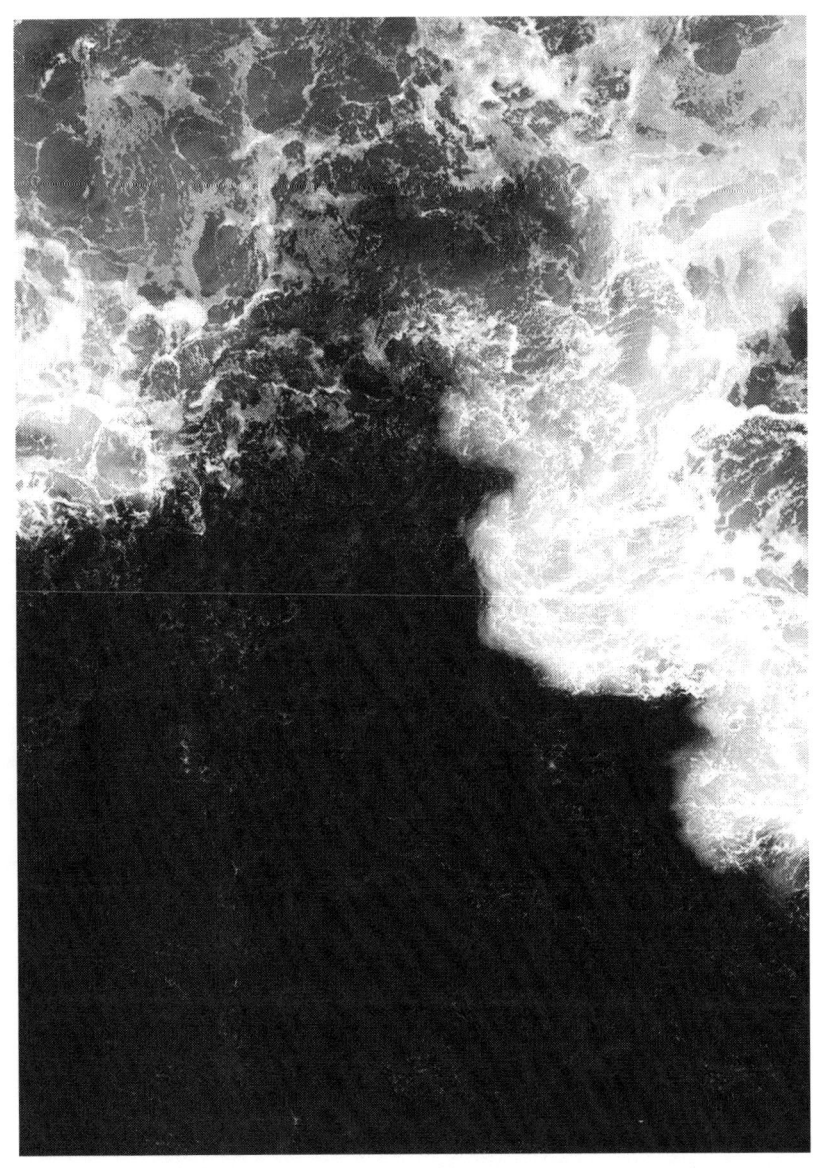

Help me

    I realize now I can't do this on my own.
I can lean on a million people to have answers
but I can't do it on my own. I need You to help
me, sustain me, and give me strength if I'm
gonna make it through this. I just got a loose
diagnosis concerning my health, of course You
know this, but I don't know what I'm doing, where
I'm going, or what's gonna happen. Regardless,
if I'm totally honest I'm scared. It's in times
like these where I feel like I just need to be
held. No one around me or myself has any idea
what's happening or what's going on it's all a
guessing game. All of our individual lives are
falling apart it seems like. Chaos has erupted
everywhere in everyone's lives it seems and
everyone's trying to manage everything, but I
feel like I can't, not on my own. I need You to
help me...

Sincerely,

Someone who needs help

Moths

Many moths have fluttered around in my garden,
although none desire to land,
They flutter around seeming as butterflies.
I desire a butterfly,
the real thing to embellish my garden.
Not some imitation that infiltrates
or bug enticed by every gaudy light in sight.
But a majestically, beautiful pollinator that
encourages the growth within.
For someday me and the King will tour,
evaluating and looking at the colors in store.
And oh, what a sight it will be
just to see the butterfly resting and awaiting me.

Gift of Faith

I decree love, joy and peace over my life.
Peace is my portion.
My long-suffering lasts.
I'm not weak or weary
but strong enough.
Please, make me strong enough.

I decree life to be in abundance in my life.
Death is defeated
and longevity of life is mine.
I'm not depressed or oppressed
but resilient.
Please, make me resilient enough.

I decree that the doors are in motion in my life.
Progress is my portion
and my future is mine.
I'm not stuck or incapable
but obedient.
Please, make me obedient enough.

The Fighting Flower

The flower grew
but nobody knew.
There's poison in the water
poured out by the prison guard.

And I heard petals
hit the ground
that never made a sound.
That never even got a chance
to echo out their hollow sound.

The foliage green
but behind the scene,
it fought just for survival,
then Papa picked me up said THRIVE.

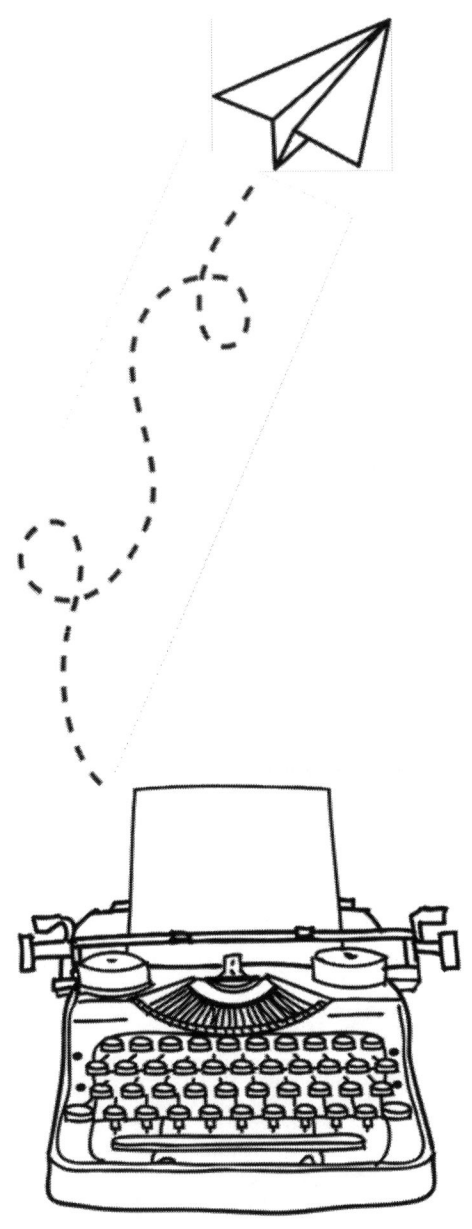

"Stay away from people

that make you feel

like you're hard to love"

~ Anonymous

How Do You Part

How do you part with a mother or a father?

How do you part with a brother or a sister?

How do you say goodbye so they can say hello?

Some get angry and break things,

some just cry while they break,

some dance for breakthrough of the unknown.

At the end of the day we all break

but there comes a time when we must heal,

recover, and stand again.

ACTION!

YET

Regardless of the circumstance,
Regardless of the situations,
Regardless of what I see
Yet, you are good.

 Regardless of the depression and oppression,
Regardless of the anxiety,
Regardless of the chaos
Yet, you are good.

Regardless of the pain,
Regardless of the sorrow,
Regardless of the drama
Yet, you are still good.

...and yet will never change.

I See You

     I have this joke that wasn't so much a joke at first but more like something deep that turned to a running joke. I would just look at someone and say, "I see you". When asked what I meant I would just repeat "I see you". I got it from a movie I was watching one day where a girl who was a celebrity jumped off the balcony of the hotel she staying in for the night in an attempt to commit suicide. When all of sudden her security guard swooped in and grabbed her by the hand as she was falling. He stared her in the eyes and said you guessed it, "I see you". Which meant I see the real you, the "you" behind all the smoke and mirrors, the mask, and the facade. That struck me right down to the core because behind all the smoke and mirrors is where the real us lies. To know that someone sees the real you is quite scary but that is where everything stems from. That person is where the healing starts. Sometimes we lose sight of the real us, ourselves. We become so good at keeping up the illusion that we even often lose track of what is real about us and what's not, or we want so bad what is true about us to not be, that we deny it even to ourselves.

Sincerely,
I see you

Game Changer

Oh love, where do I begin. I know let's start with simply… I love you. I know you may not understand now but I do and I always will. We may not always agree but never forget I will always be on your team. I will always try to be the loudest one screaming when you need a cheerleader, the tightest hug when you need one and the most understanding and wise when you need help or want to talk. When your parents told me about you, I never felt such a love instantly for another human, especially one I hadn't met yet. Until that point I have raised a couple of kids, had a couple God-brothers and a God-sister, and I had watched our family grow and people get new titles like; Aunt, Uncle, Grandma, Grandpa but I was always still a cousin when it came to blood family, (don't worry I later realized the power of my name and what it really meant). But it all changed when your parents called me "FUNCLE" and though I doubted and questioned my made up title your mother snapped me in line when it came its meaning. She said, "You are my brother and he is your nephew, you can go by whatever you want, but that will never change," and from that moment on my love for you grew so much stronger. No matter

what may happen or what may come just know I will
always love you and that will never change.

If I could leave you with anything it would
be the following. Family is family no matter
what and we have to be there for each other
because one day some of us won't be here anymore.
No matter how bad someone hurts you, walk in
love even though it may hurt more than anything
forgive them and then love them, that's what
makes you the bigger person. More than anything
I want you to always remember that hurting people
hurt people and broken people will try to break
other people but a person who truly loves you
wants the best for you even if it hurts them in
the process.

I Love You,

Your Funcle

Made in the USA
Middletown, DE
11 January 2026

26896634R00123